W9-BYF-747

One-Pan Meals

SHEET PAN AND SKILLET DINNERS
FOR THE WHOLE FAMILY

TAREQ TAYLOR
Translated by Ellen Hedström

Skyhorse Publishing

CONTENTS

THE OVEN—
YOUR HOUSEHOLD FRIEND

I'm frequently asked how to simplify home cooking. One of the most common questions I get is, "Do you have a book with a few really good, simple recipes that I can pass on to my kids who are leaving home?" Of course, I have many recipes for anyone who is daunted by this task! However, there is one thing that I have not used enough of and that can actually make cooking much easier for everyone—the oven.

We usually use the oven to bake or make casseroles now and then, but there is so much more you can do with it. You can grill, roast, fry, boil, bake, cure, broil, and more in a simple oven. In addition, using an oven allows the food to cook itself, giving you time to do other things away from the stove. (Though personally I think any time spent at the stove is an investment rather than a waste.)

There is a great joy and many health benefits in a good home-cooked meal based on raw ingredients. However, I also understand that we sometimes wish there is a quicker and easier way to get food on the table.

That's why I've filled this book with a variety of tasty and effortless dishes that can be made in the oven—everything from healthy, crunchy granola to savory dinners that will make life simpler and better-tasting, whether you are a professional or just an enthusiastic beginner. Of course, these quick and easy recipes work just as well at dinner parties or for a special dinner for two. You will also find recipes and tips on how to bake your own amazing sourdough bread and the perfect pizza.

It's finally here—one-pan meals.
Happy cooking!

OVENS, PANS, OVENWARE, PAPER, FOIL . . .

Whatever you cook or bake in the oven takes care of itself and needs little attention. To cook your meal in a pan, there are a few things you need. First, you need an oven, preferably a convection oven.

You also need sheet pans, a roasting pan, and an oven rack to place smaller dishes on (in some recipes I use other types of ovenware instead of a sheet pan). You can decide if you want to use parchment paper for your pan or dish or use butter or oil to grease it, but note that there's less washing up with parchment paper.

THE OVEN

Obviously, every oven is different, which is why it is important to get to know your own oven. Depending on the oven, the recommended temperatures in this cookbook can mean that the food will either brown too quickly or not cook fast enough.

An oven that is not self-cleaning can be cleaned using different methods, such as with baking powder, water, and vinegar or with dishwashing liquid and water. You'll find many good tips on the Internet if you search "cleaning your oven."

CONVECTION OVENS

In a convection or fan-assisted oven, air circulates inside the oven so that the heat is evenly distributed. The symbol for a convection oven is a circle with an illustration of a fan inside it. Temperatures should be the same throughout the whole convection oven, so you can put several sheet pans on different oven racks at the same time. It also shouldn't matter where you place the tray in the oven.

If you have a recommended temperature of around 390°F for a "normal" conventional oven—with top and bottom heat elements—you can reduce it by about 70°F for a convection oven. The recipes in this book are for a convection oven, so if you don't have one, you'll need to slightly increase the temperatures you cook at.

Another good thing about a convection oven is that is requires less energy than an oven that uses top and bottom heat. Ovens with the heating element by the fan have the best fan-assisted effect.

PANS

Modern pans are often enamel or have a nonstick surface. They can have low edges (a sheet pan or baking pan) or slightly higher edges (a roasting pan). Pans usually manage an oven temperature of up to 570°F.

A dirty pan can be hard to clean, especially if you used butter or oil to grease it. Luckily, there are some cleaning tricks.

REMEMBER!

Don't start heating the oven too soon so it is left on unnecessarily.

Turn the oven off just a bit before the food is ready to utilize the remaining heat to finish the cooking process.

Parchment paper can be recycled a few times, for example, after you have made bread or cookies.

Here are my best tips to clean your pans. Scrub it with dishwashing liquid and leave it in the oven at 210°F for around 15 minutes to loosen the dirt. You can also pour vinegar in the pan and leave it in the oven at 120°F for a few hours. Make sure you have good ventilation in your kitchen as vinegar has a strong smell. Another way to wash your pans is to mix a few tablespoons of baking powder with water to make a paste. Smear the paste over the pan and leave it for 12 hours, then wash with dishwashing liquid.

Remember that pans can buckle and warp from big temperature changes, such as if you pour cold water on a hot tray, so be careful, especially when you use your best pan!

OVENWARE

The most important thing when cooking with an oven is to find a vessel that is oven-safe at a high heat. The following materials work well—stainless steel, heatproof glass, ceramic, or cast iron. Most ovenware can go in the dishwasher except cast iron, which should be cleaned under running water.

PARCHMENT PAPER

A sheet of parchment paper can be placed on the sheet pan or in the roasting pan to make sure food doesn't stick. This means you don't need to grease the pan, which will make it easier to clean.

Parchment paper, which is made from cellulose, is available in white or brown and can be smooth or have some texture. Note that greaseproof paper, which looks similar, shouldn't be used instead of parchment paper; despite being resilient to fat, it doesn't work at high temperatures.

Remember, too, that parchment paper can catch fire if it touches the heating element, so be careful!

If you want to be able to remove a cake or pie easily, place parchment paper between the base and ring of a springform pan.

SILICONE MATS AND OTHER BAKING MATS

A silicone mat acts like parchment paper, ensuring that food doesn't stick to the pan during baking. A silicone mat can withstand high heat and be reused once it's been washed with dishwashing liquid. There are also baking mats made from other materials that can be recycled and used again.

ALUMINUM FOIL

A thin foil made from aluminum can be used to cover food when baking or in place of cellophane wrap to protect food when stored in the fridge. Aluminum foil has a matte side and a shiny side. The shiny side reflects heat slightly better, but generally it doesn't matter which way up it should be placed.

If I am baking something in a foil packet, I always place parchment paper as a double layer on the inside of the foil since the foil can sometimes leak aluminum. I prefer not to place food directly on top of aluminum foil.

There are different types of aluminum foil, with slightly thicker varieties meant for the oven or freezer and thinner varieties to protect food when stored in the fridge.

In the packaging of aluminum foil, you should see a small tab on each end of the box. These should be pressed inward to keep the roll in place and allow for easy tearing of the foil.

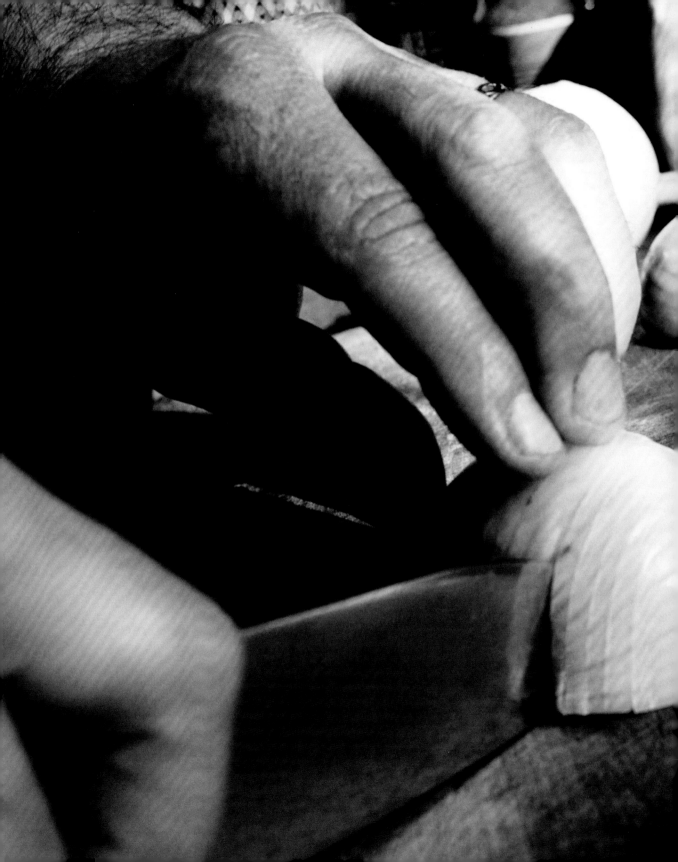

VEGETABLES

MUSHROOM AND ZUCCHINI FRITTATA

To make the frittata more filling, cut up any leftover boiled potatoes you have and place them at the bottom of the pan. You can also cut 2 to 3 small uncooked potatoes into very thin slices (preferably using a mandoline) and place them on top of all the other ingredients before the pan goes into the oven.

1. Heat a convection oven to 356°F.
2. Peel and slice the onion. Peel and chop the garlic. Slice the mushrooms into quarters and dice the yellow summer squash and zucchini.
3. Fry the onion, garlic, mushrooms, squash, and zucchini in olive oil together with salt and thyme in an oven-safe frying pan for a few minutes.
4. Whisk the eggs with water, parsley, salt, and pepper in a bowl. Pour the egg mixture over the mixture in the pan and place in the oven. Cook the frittata for around 10 minutes.
5. Remove from the oven and serve immediately with a mixed green salad (optional).

SERVES 4

1 yellow onion
1 clove garlic
4 mushrooms
1 medium yellow summer squash
1 medium zucchini
1 tablespoon olive oil
1 teaspoon flaked salt
2 teaspoons finely chopped fresh thyme
6 eggs
⅕ cup water
⅖ cup chopped parsley
1 teaspoon salt
Freshly ground black pepper

TOMATO, PEPPER, AND CHILI STEW

This is a Basque vegetable stew called *piperade* that is similar to a French ratatouille and just as versatile. It's great on its own with just some sourdough bread on the side—or as a sauce on top of fresh pasta with a little Parmesan and capers.

1. Heat a convection oven to 527°F.
2. Halve the peppers and cut into strips. Peel and halve the onion and slice into strips. Slice the chili with its seeds. Cut the tomatoes into wedges.
3. Place everything in an oven-safe dish. Pour in the oil, season with salt, and mix.
4. Bake in the oven for 25 minutes, stirring a few times during baking.
5. Remove the dish from the oven and sprinkle with fresh oregano. Stir and serve immediately with sourdough bread (optional).

SERVES 4

2 green, yellow, or red bell peppers
1 yellow onion
1 red chili pepper
4 tomatoes on the vine
⅔ cup olive oil
3 teaspoons salt
Fresh oregano leaves

WHITE BEANS
IN TOMATO SAUCE

Add a piece of salt pork or bacon to the sauce and cook it with the beans to give it a deeper, richer flavor.

1. Soak the beans in cold water for at least 12 hours.
2. Heat a convection oven to 392°F.
3. Mix crushed tomatoes, tomato puree, bouillon stock powder or a crumbled stock cube, water, lemon juice, and salt in a bowl. Mix with a hand blender to make a smooth sauce.
4. Peel and halve the onion.
5. Drain the beans and place them in an oven-safe casserole dish with a lid. Pour in the tomato sauce and add the onion halves. Place the lid on top and bake in the oven for around 2 hours.
6. Remove from the oven and serve immediately. I usually eat these beans with some fried sausage or bacon, toast, fried potatoes, or whole baked tomatoes.

SERVES 4

Around 1 pound dried white beans
Cold water to soak the beans
3 cups crushed tomatoes, around 2 cans
3 tablespoons tomato puree
1 teaspoon bouillon stock powder or ½ chicken stock cube
⅖ cup water
Freshly squeezed juice from ½ lemon
2 teaspoons salt
1 yellow onion

STUFFED PORTOBELLO WITH CHEESE

Portobello is a brown mushroom that has grown very large. Its huge cap is perfect for stuffing or filling, just like we do in this recipe.

1. Heat a convection oven to 356°F.
2. Cut the stalks off the mushrooms and place the caps to the side for later. Finely chop the stalks. Peel and finely chop the onion and garlic.
3. Cut the crusts off the bread and discard, and cut or crumble the remaining bread into small pieces. Remove the leaves from the thyme, retaining the sprigs.
4. Heat the butter in a frying pan and fry the sliced mushroom stalks and onion and garlic together with the bread crumbs and thyme leaves for a few minutes.
5. Place the mushrooms on the pan with the gills on the underside of the caps facing up. Evenly distribute the mix from the frying pan inside the caps. Top them off with grated cheese and salt and place the thyme sprigs on the pan. Bake in the oven for around 25 minutes.
6. Remove from the oven and serve immediately. Feel free to add a mixed green salad and some sourdough bread.

SERVES 4

4 large portobello mushrooms, around 2.2 pounds
1 yellow onion
2 garlic cloves
1 large slice sourdough bread
10 sprigs fresh thyme
1 tablespoon butter
1⅓ cups grated hard, strong cow's cheese, such as aged Parmesan, cheddar, or Västerbotten
1 teaspoon flaked salt

INDIAN CAULIFLOWER CASSEROLE WITH POMEGRANATE SALAD

I love Indian food! In this casserole, you'll find garam masala, turmeric, and cumin—all typical ingredients from an Indian kitchen.

SERVES 4

1 head cauliflower, around 1.7 pounds

SAUCE

1.7 ounces cashew nuts
⅘ cup Greek yogurt for cooking
⅗ cup water
1 peeled garlic clove
2 teaspoons garam masala
1 teaspoon turmeric
1 teaspoon ground cumin
½ teaspoon coriander seeds
1 teaspoon salt

POMEGRANATE SALAD

Seeds from ½ pomegranate
⅕ cup raisins
¼ yellow onion, thinly sliced
⅕ cup fresh flat-leaf parsley leaves
⅕ cup fresh cilantro
1 tablespoon freshly pressed lemon juice
2 teaspoons pomegranate syrup
2 teaspoons olive oil

1. Heat a convection oven to 356°F.
2. Break the cauliflower up into large florets and place into an oven-safe dish.
3. Mix all the ingredients for the sauce. Pour the sauce over the cauliflower and place the dish in the oven. Bake for about 30 minutes.
4. To make the pomegranate salad, mix the pomegranate seeds, raisins, onion, parsley, and cilantro in a dish. Pour over the lemon juice, pomegranate syrup, and olive oil and mix.
5. Remove the cauliflower from the oven and cover with the salad. Serve immediately.

BEETS WITH FETA
AND PINE NUTS

I've always loved beets! They really shine in this recipe together with feta, pine nuts (which in botanical terms are actually seeds), and lots of fresh oregano. A modern classic! If you can't find crema di balsamico, you can use balsamic vinegar, though they are not the same—the former is creamier than the latter.

1. Heat a convection oven to 356°F.
2. Peel the beets and cut into wedges. Place them in a pan and pour in olive oil. Add salt and mix. Roast in the oven for about 30 minutes.
3. Remove the pan from the oven and evenly distribute the pine nuts over the beets. Place the pan in the oven again and roast for about 5 minutes to brown the nuts.
4. Remove the pan from the oven and crumble in the feta cheese. Top with fresh oregano and drizzle some crema di balsamico or balsamic vinegar over it. Serve immediately either as a starter or as a side dish to something grilled or baked.

SERVES 4

1½ pounds beets
3 tablespoons olive oil
½ teaspoon salt
1.7 ounces pine nuts
3.5 ounces feta cheese
Fresh oregano to garnish
1 tablespoon crema di
    balsamico or balsamic
    vinegar

BUTTERNUT SQUASH AND ZUCCHINI WITH CAPERS, ALMONDS, AND RAISINS

This is a complex little dish filled with color—the almond adds texture and the ricotta adds creaminess. The sweetness of the roasted squash and tartness of the capers is an excellent combination, in my opinion.

1. Heat a convection oven to 356°F.
2. Peel and cut the butternut squash into ¾-inch pieces. Halve the summer squash and zucchini lengthwise. Cut the halves into quarters about the same size as the butternut squash pieces. Peel and finely chop the garlic cloves.
3. Place the zucchini and squash pieces on a pan. Pour the chopped garlic, rosemary leaves, and almonds evenly on top. Season with salt and pepper. Finish off by drizzling olive oil over it and mixing. Roast in the oven for about 35 minutes.
4. Remove the pan from the oven and top with dollops of ricotta, as well as the raisins and capers. Serve immediately with some grilled fish such as tuna, salmon, or cod.

SERVES 4

0.8 pounds butternut squash
0.8 pounds yellow summer squash and zucchini
2 garlic cloves
Leaves from a sprig of fresh rosemary
1.7 ounces almonds
½ teaspoon salt
Freshly ground pepper
2 tablespoons olive oil
8.8 ounces ricotta
⅖ cup raisins
10–12 large capers

BUTTERNUT SQUASH WITH ONION, HAZELNUTS, AND DUKKAH

Dukkah is an Egyptian spice mix that is available in several varieties and very easy to make. Here is my very own version!

1. Warm a convection oven to 356°F.
2. Peel and cut the squash into fairly large pieces. Peel and cut the onion in half and separate the layers.
3. Evenly spread the squash and onion in a baking pan and drizzle with olive oil. Mix and roast in the oven for around 30 minutes.
4. Meanwhile, roast all ingredients for the dukkah in a dry frying pan until they start to smell good. Crush the seeds and spices with a pestle and mortar.
5. Remove the pan from the oven and sprinkle the dukkah and hazelnuts over the squash. Garnish with lemon balm or lemon zest and serve immediately. This is a perfect accompaniment to grilled meat, gnocchi, or cooked lentils that provides lots of flavor.

SERVES 4

1.4 pounds butternut squash
1 yellow onion
1–2 tablespoons olive oil
1 ounce roasted hazelnuts
Lemon balm or lemon zest to garnish

DUKKAH

⅔ cup white sesame seeds
1 teaspoon dill seeds
½ teaspoon chili flakes
½ teaspoon lemon pepper
1½ teaspoon whole black pepper

BAKED WHOLE CELERIAC WITH GARLIC BUTTER

Don't shy away from the color of this butter—it tastes amazing, I promise! Aged or black garlic, which can be found in larger grocery stores, adds color as well as a flavor of balsamic vinegar to the butter.

1. Heat a convection oven to 428°F.
2. Clean the celeriac but keep the skin on. Cut off the base by the roots and place the celeriac, with the cut edge facing down, on a pan lined with parchment paper. Bake in the oven for about an hour or until the inside temperature is 200°F.
3. Meanwhile mix butter, garlic, salt, and lemon juice with a hand blender to make a smooth, brown butter.
4. Remove the celeriac from the oven and place upside down on a plate. Add a large dollop of garlic butter in the hole that has formed in the bottom. Garnish with tarragon and chervil or parsley and serve immediately with a piece of roast meat. It also works as a vegetarian dish with lentils.

SERVES 4

1 celeriac, around 1.7 pounds
Fresh tarragon and chervil or
   parsley to garnish

GARLIC BUTTER

3.5 ounces butter at room
   temperature
0.8 ounces fermented garlic
Salt
1 teaspoon fresh lemon juice

ZUCCHINI WITH TOMATO, GREEN PEPPER, AND CHILI

This was the dish that made me love zucchini. I had never really appreciated the relatively tasteless vegetable before. This recipe is my father's and is now a classic in our house!

1. Heat a convection oven to 356°F.
2. Peel and chop the onion. Halve and slice the bell peppers into coarse pieces and the chili pepper into small pieces. Cut the zucchini and tomatoes into ⅓-inch slices.
3. Fry the onion, pepper, and chili in most of the olive oil in a casserole with a lid. Place the zucchini and then the tomatoes in layers over the rest of the vegetables. Season with salt and pepper. Place the lid on the dish and put in the oven to bake for an hour.
4. Peel and chop the garlic cloves, and fry in a little bit of olive oil together with the coriander in a small saucepan.
5. Remove the casserole from the oven and pour the garlic and coriander in oil over the vegetables. Serve immediately on its own or with cooked rice or sourdough bread.

SERVES 4

1 yellow onion
2 green bell peppers
1 red or green chili pepper
2 zucchini
1.1 pounds fresh tomatoes
⅔ cup olive oil, divided
Salt
Freshly ground pepper
2 garlic cloves
1 teaspoon ground coriander

LENTIL-STUFFED VEGETABLES WITH SPINACH SALAD

Here's my offering of a typical seventies dish that I think deserves to be revived. The dish is completely vegetarian and works just as well today as it did then.

1. Make the ground lentils using the recipe on page 37, then add chopped chili and cumin.
2. Heat a convection oven to 356°F.
3. Halve the summer squash. Cut the tops off the peppers and tomatoes like a lid, then use a spoon or the back of a potato peeler to hollow out the vegetables by removing the flesh and setting it aside. Take the flesh from the tomatoes and summer squash and mix it with the lentils. Then, stuff the hollowed-out vegetables with the mixture.
4. Place the stuffed vegetables on a pan with parchment paper. Halve the lemon and place on the pan. Cook everything in the oven for about 45 minutes.
5. When the vegetables are almost done, prepare the spinach salad. Peel and dice the red onion. Halve the cucumber lengthwise and cut into half-moon shapes. Chop the mint and cilantro. Mix the onion, cucumber, mint, cilantro, lime juice, and oil. Fold the spinach into this mix.
6. Remove the vegetables from the oven and squeeze the baked lemon halves on top. Serve immediately together with the salad.

SERVES 4

1 yellow summer squash
2 green or red bell peppers
4 tomatoes
1 lemon

GROUND LENTILS

Ground lentils (see page 37)
1 red chili pepper, chopped
1 tsp ground cumin

SPINACH SALAD

½ red onion
4-inch cucumber
1 small bunch mint
1 small bunch cilantro
Juice from 1 lime
1 tablespoon olive oil
2.5 ounces baby spinach

EGGPLANT WITH TOMATO AND GROUND LENTILS

Soaking the lentils takes about one hour. Other than that, this vegetarian version of ground meat is both quick and easy to make.

1. Prepare the ground lentils first. Soak the lentils in plenty of cold water for at least an hour. Drain and discard the water.
2. Heat a convection oven to 356°F.
3. Peel and chop the onion coarsely. Peel the garlic. Chop onion, garlic, parsley, and thyme in a food processor or with a handheld blender. Add the lentils and process to a fairly smooth texture. Add lemon and salt and pepper to taste.
4. Cut the eggplant into ¼-inch slices.
5. Oil an oven dish or pan and spread out the ground lentils. Cover with the eggplant slices. Pour the crushed tomato on top and season with salt and pepper. Drizzle with some olive oil and bake in the oven for around 30 minutes.
6. Remove from the oven and serve immediately with a mixed green salad and sourdough bread.

SERVES 4

½ eggplant
5 tablespoons olive oil, divided
1 can crushed tomatoes, around 1 pound
Salt
Freshly ground pepper

GROUND LENTILS

0.8 pounds red lentils
Water to soak the lentils
1 yellow onion
2 garlic cloves
⅔ cup fresh flat-leaf parsley
2 tablespoons fresh thyme leaves
1 tablespoon fresh lemon juice
Salt
Freshly ground pepper

EGGPLANT WITH HALLOUMI AND ZA'ATAR

Za'atar is a spice mix or paste from the Middle East and North Africa that usually contains sesame seeds, sumac, and Syrian oregano. It is usually mixed into olive oil, which makes it really tasty when brushed over pita bread or fried or grilled lamb.

1. Heat a convection oven to 356°F.
2. Cut the eggplants into roughly ¾-inch slices. Halve the tomatoes and lemon. Cut the halloumi into 1-inch cubes. Peel and halve the garlic cloves lengthwise.
3. Place the eggplant slices in a large baking or roasting pan. Place the tomatoes and halloumi evenly on top. Place the lemon halves (with the cut side facing up) and the garlic cloves on top. Drizzle some olive oil over the top and season with salt and pepper. Roast in the oven for around 30 minutes.
4. Remove the pan from the oven and sprinkle za'tar and more olive oil on top. Squeeze a lemon half over the dish and mix. Serve immediately with sourdough bread and/or a mixed green salad, or as a side dish to grilled chicken.

SERVES 4

2 eggplants
4 tomatoes
1 lemon
0.5 pound halloumi
2 garlic cloves
3 tablespoons olive oil, divided
2 teaspoons coarse salt
Freshly ground black pepper
1 tablespoon za'atar

SWEET POTATO WITH BROCCOLI, FETA, AND POMEGRANATE SEEDS

The beautiful, vibrantly orange sweet potato is here to stay. Sweet potatoes are in fact not related to potatoes at all. The tuberous root of the sweet potato is often used for cooking, but you can also eat the leaves.

1. Heat a convection oven to 356°F.
2. Cut the eggplant into pieces. Place the pieces on a plate and salt with approximately 1 teaspoon of salt.
3. Peel and cut the sweet potato into pieces. Mix with five-spice powder, flaked salt, and around 1 tablespoon olive oil.
4. Cut the broccoli florets from the stem. Thinly peel the stem and cut into slices. Mix the florets and slices with around 1 tablespoon olive oil and 1 teaspoon salt.
5. Place the eggplant, sweet potato, and broccoli pieces on a pan. Add cumin and mix. Roast in the oven for around 30 minutes. Remove from the oven and pour the pine nuts evenly on top. Roast for another 15 minutes (total cooking time is 45 minutes).
6. Meanwhile, scoop out the pomegranate. It's easiest to do this if you hold the halved fruit with the cut side facing down over a bowl and then tap it with the back of a ladle to make the seeds fall out. Set the seeds aside.
7. Remove the pan from the oven and crumble bits of feta cheese over the vegetables. Top with pomegranate seeds and flat-leaf. Squeeze some lemon juice on top and serve immediately, on its own as a vegetarian dish with a mixed green salad or as an accompaniment to roast chicken.

SERVES 4

1 eggplant
Around 2 teaspoons salt, divided
1.5 pounds sweet potato
½ teaspoon five-spice powder
Around 1 teaspoon flaked salt
2–3 tablespoons olive oil, divided
1 bunch broccoli
½ teaspoon ground cumin
2.5 ounces pine nuts
½ pomegranate
3.5 ounces feta cheese
1 small bunch flat-leaf parsley, leaves finely diced
½ lemon

CORN ON THE COB WITH SRIRACHA MAYONNAISE AND CHEESE

The first time I tasted this was when I was filming *Kockarnas Kamp 2017* (Best Chef 2017) and chef Jonas Svensson served us this absolutely delicious but simple corn. You have to use store-bought sriracha mayonnaise.

1. Heat a convection oven to 437°F.
2. Place the corn in a pan and drizzle with sriracha mayonnaise. Top it off with grated cheese and drizzle with even more sriracha mayonnaise if you like!
3. Roast in the oven for around 20 minutes. Serve immediately.

SERVES 4

4 ears of corn on the cob, husked
Sriracha mayonnaise, an embarrassing amount!
3.5 ounces grated hard, strong cow's cheese, such as aged Parmesan, cheddar, or Västerbotten

POTATO GRATIN
WITH GOAT CHEESE

Potato gratin is the best thing ever—especially as a meal during fall and winter. Apart from adding salsify in the gratin, I've elevated the flavors with goat cheese and rosemary. If you don't have salsify, you can substitute it with parsnips. Try it—it's excellent with lamb!

1. Heat a convection oven to 356°F.
2. Peel the potato and cut into ¼-inch slices. Peel and slice the salsify or parsnip into thick slices.
3. Layer the potato and salsify in an oven-safe dish and add salt. Pull the rosemary leaves off the sprig and sprinkle over the gratin. Top with dollops of goat cheese and pour cream over everything. Bake in the oven for around 45 minutes.
4. Remove from the oven and serve immediately as an accompaniment to the herbed pork tenderloin on page 82 or to the roast lamb on page 102.

4 SERVINGS

1.1 pounds potato
1 large salsify or parsnip
1 teaspoon salt
2 sprigs fresh rosemary
3.5 ounces goat cheese
1⅖ cup whipping cream

FISH AND SEAFOOD

HERB-STUFFED TROUT WITH ZUCCHINI CASSEROLE

Zucchini casserole straight from the oven

Trout is an easy fish to prepare and is much better cooked whole rather than as a fillet. When it's cooked whole, the bones loosen almost by themselves, making them easy to remove.

1. Heat a convection oven to 392°F.
2. Stuff the trout with parsley, dill, and slices of lemon. Add salt and pepper both inside and outside the fish. Place the fish on a pan lined with parchment paper, leaving some space on the pan for the zucchini casserole.
3. Cut the zucchini into thin slices, preferably using a mandoline, around 0.1-inch thick.
4. Mix crème fraîche, cream, lemon zest, lemon juice, salt, and thyme.
5. Start by layering zucchini slices at the bottom of an oven-safe dish that can fit on the pan. Then add a second layer of the crème fraîche mixture. Keep layering, and finally finish off with the crème fraîche mixture on top.
6. Place the dish on the pan with the fish and put everything in the oven. Bake the fish and zucchini at the same time for around 20 minutes.
7. Remove from the oven and serve the fish immediately with the zucchini.

SERVES 4

2 whole trout, gutted
1 small bunch parsley
1 small bunch dill
1 lemon, sliced
Salt
Freshly ground pepper

ZUCCHINI CASSEROLE

Just over 0.6 pound zucchini
⅕ cup crème fraîche
⅔ cup whipping cream
Grated zest from ½ lemon
2 teaspoons freshly squeezed
   lemon juice
½ teaspoon salt
1 teaspoon finely chopped
   fresh thyme

MACKEREL FILLETS WITH VEGETABLES, LEMON, AND CAPERS

Mackerel is one of my favorite fish. It has a nice, firm flesh and a fantastic taste. It also works very well with Mediterranean flavors and ingredients like tomato, capers, and lemon.

1. Heat the oven to 392°F using the grill function (bottom heat).
2. Peel and finely dice the onion. Dice the zucchini, eggplant, and pepper. Halve the tomatoes and roughly chop the capers and olives. Mix the chopped and cut vegetables with lemon zest. Add salt and pepper.
3. Place the vegetables on a plate and place the mackerel on top. Grill in the oven for around 7 minutes.
4. Remove from the oven and serve immediately with a mixed green salad and maybe a glass of white wine.

SERVES 4

½ yellow onion
3.5 ounces zucchini
3.5 ounces eggplant
½ red bell pepper
10 cherry tomatoes
10 giant capers
20 kalamata olives, seeds removed
Finely grated zest from 1 lemon
Salt
Freshly ground pepper
4 mackerel fillets

WHOLE MACKEREL WITH CURRY VEGETABLES

The mild curry-flavored vegetables
work perfectly with the mackerel

"The first time I encountered this way of eating mackerel was in the Seychelles. The scores in the fish create sections in the flesh that, once cooked, are easy to pull off for a piece of fish without many bones."

1. Heat a convection oven to 356°F.
2. Score the fish, like in the photo. Peel the garlic cloves and then finely chop the cloves and chili. Mix garlic, chili, oil, and salt and rub the fish with the mixture. Place on a pan lined with parchment paper.
3. To make the curry vegetables, peel and coarsely chop the red onion. Cut the scallions, chili, and zucchini into equal sizes. Mix the cut vegetables, lemon juice, tomato puree, curry, coconut milk, water, and salt in an oven-safe dish. Bake in the oven for around 15 minutes.
4. Then place the pan with the mackerel in the oven and bake everything for a further 20 minutes (a total cooking time of around 35 minutes for the vegetables).
5. Remove from the oven and serve immediately with cooked jasmine rice. To debone the fish, first remove the flesh from the top or according to the way it is scored. Then remove the whole backbone, starting from the tail fin and pulling it out until you reach the head, so the bottom flesh can also be eaten.

SERVES 4

2 whole mackerel
2 garlic cloves
½ red chili pepper
1 tablespoon olive oil
Salt

CURRY VEGETABLES

1 red onion
2 scallions
1 red chili pepper
1 yellow zucchini
Freshly squeezed juice from
    ½ lemon
2 tablespoons tomato puree
4 tablespoons curry
⅘ cup coconut milk
⅘ cup water
2 teaspoons salt

SALMON PUDDING WITH MELTED BUTTER AND HORSERADISH

A favorite dish that I make again and again. For me, it's obvious to serve salmon pudding with melted butter, freshly grated horseradish, and freshly squeezed lemon on top. If you don't have horseradish, you can get the flavor from horseradish sauce or mustard.

1. Heat a convection oven to 356°F.
2. Cut the potatoes and fresh salmon fillets, smoked salmon, and cured salmon into ¼-inch slices. Layer the salmon and potatoes in an oven-safe dish.
3. Finely chop the dill and chives. Whisk the dill and chives together with egg, milk, cream, and salt. Pour the mixture over the potatoes and salmon and bake in the oven for around 40 minutes.
4. Remove and squeeze lemon juice over the dish. Finish off with grated horseradish and serve immediately with melted butter in a separate dish.

SERVES 4

4–6 cold potatoes, peeled
Around 1 pound fresh salmon fillets
Around 3.5 ounces fresh, cold smoked salmon
Around 3.5 ounces cured salmon (gravlax or lox)
1 large bunch dill, stalks and leaves
1 bunch chives
5 eggs
1¾ cup whole milk
⅖ cup whipping cream
2 teaspoons salt

TO SERVE

½ lemon
1 large piece horseradish, grated
3.5 ounces melted butter

SALMON SKEWERS THREE WAYS WITH PICKLED VEGETABLES

This teriyaki salmon tastes even better if you mix the pickled bean sprouts with a little wakame seaweed. If you want to make it even simpler, oven-bake a whole salmon, skin on, with one of the flavorings of your choice.

1. Heat the oven to 392°F, top heat.
2. Make the pickled cucumber. Halve the cucumber lengthwise and discard the center section with seeds. Slice the cucumber very thinly and place them in a bowl. Massage in the salt with your hands and squeeze the cucumber to remove its liquid. Cut the carrot into very thin slices, preferably using a mandoline. Mix the cucumber and carrot with sugar and vinegar.
3. Make the pickled bean sprouts. Place the bean sprouts in a bowl and add salt. Leave for a few minutes to remove liquid. Then mix with salt, sesame oil, garlic, scallions, and chives.
4. Cut the salmon into large square pieces, around 1½-inch cubes Place the pieces on skewers and put them on a pan lined with parchment paper.
5. Prepare the skewers three ways with three flavorings. First, mix the tandoori spice and yogurt in a small bowl. Then, brush the tandoori yogurt mixture onto one-third of the salmon skewers. Cover another one-third of the salmon skewers with dukkah. Finally, brush teriyaki sauce on the remaining salmon skewers and add sesame seeds.
6. Bake the salmon skewers in the oven for around 10 minutes. Remove the pan from the oven midway through and dip the skewers that were brushed with teriyaki sauce in any extra sauce that has leaked onto the parchment paper. Sprinkle the teriyaki skewers with roasted sesame seeds.
7. Serve the skewers warm with pickled vegetables. Garnish with cilantro or another herb.

SERVES 4

1.3 pounds salmon fillet without skin
Cilantro or another herb to garnish

PICKLED CUCUMBER

1 cucumber
1 teaspoon fine salt
½ small carrot
¼ cup sugar
¼ cup rice or white wine vinegar

PICKLED BEAN SPROUTS

1 pint fresh bean sprouts
½ teaspoon salt
2 teaspoons sesame oil
½ garlic clove, grated
1 scallion, finely sliced
1 tablespoon finely chopped chives

FLAVORINGS

1 tablespoon tandoori spice + 2 tablespoons Greek yogurt
4 teaspoons dukkah (see page 29)
2 tablespoons teriyaki sauce + approx. 1 teaspoon roasted sesame seeds

COD FILLET WITH CELERIAC CASSEROLE AND ASPARAGUS

A simple version of a fish casserole where I use celeriac instead of potato. This is a really good weekday meal, which is given an extra edge by the asparagus.

1. Heat a convection oven to 392°F.
2. Peel the celeriac and cut into ½-inch cubes. Pluck the tarragon leaves from its sprig and cut into pieces.
3. Place the diced celeriac into an oven-safe dish. Mix the cream with tarragon and salt and pour the mixture over the celeriac. Place the dish on a pan and bake in the oven for around 20 minutes.
4. Remove the dish from the oven and place the cod on top.
5. Break off the lower, thicker part of the asparagus stalks (they should break naturally). Place the stalks on parchment paper on the same pan as the dish with the cod and drizzle with some oil. Return the pan to the oven and bake everything for another 10 minutes.
6. Remove from the oven and sprinkle with flaked salt and freshly ground pepper. Serve immediately.

SERVES 4

Around 1 pound celeriac
1 small bunch fresh tarragon
⅖ cup whipping cream
½ teaspoon salt
Around 1 pound cod fillet
12 asparagus spears
1 tablespoon olive oil
Flaked salt
Freshly ground black pepper

COD WITH CREAMY ANCHOVY AND HERB CASSEROLE

This is a fish casserole with the taste of Jansson's temptation (an anchovy and potato dish usually served during Christmas in Sweden). But why not eat it midweek, way before Christmas? Feel free to serve with a cold beer!

1. Heat a convection oven to 392°F.
2. Prepare the casserole. Discard the brine from the anchovies and finely chop the fillets. Finely chop the dill and chives. Mix the anchovies and dill and chives with crème fraîche, cream, lemon zest, lemon juice, and salt.
3. Break the potato into pieces and place them along the edges of an oven-safe dish.
4. Place the cod or other whitefish in the middle and pour the sauce over. Bake in the oven until the casserole is a nice color, around 15 to 20 minutes.
5. Remove from the oven and drizzle with fresh dill. Serve immediately with a mixed green salad and lemon wedges.

SERVES 4

8 cold potatoes, peeled
1.3 pounds cod fillet or another whitefish
A few bunches good quality dill to serve
½ lemon to serve

ANCHOVIES AND HERB CASSEROLE

1 pack anchovy fillets, around 4 ounces
1 small bunch dill
1 small bunch chives
⅘ cup crème fraîche
⅖ cup whipping cream
Finely grated zest from 1 lemon
2 tablespoons freshly squeezed lemon juice
1 teaspoon flaked salt

COD WITH
TOMATO AND BASIL

A lovely fish dish with simple but very tasty Italian flavors. Smash the tomatoes slightly when you take the dish out of the oven to make it juicy and delicious.

1. Heat a convection oven to 356°F.
2. Cut the tomatoes in half. Place in an oven-safe dish. Place the fish on top and drizzle with olive oil. Add salt. Bake in the oven for around 20 minutes.
3. Meanwhile, pluck the basil leaves from the sprig and chop roughly.
4. Remove the pan from the oven, sprinkle the basil over the dish, and serve immediately. This tastes good with cooked spaghetti or gnocchi that will soak up the lovely juices. You can also squeeze lemon juice over it.

SERVES 4

4 ripe tomatoes
4 pieces cod fillet, around
    3.5 ounces each, with
    skin on
3 tablespoons olive oil
1 teaspoon salt
1 bunch fresh basil

TO SERVE

Lemon wedges (optional)

FOIL PACKET COD WITH VEGETABLES AND DILL BUTTER

It doesn't get any simpler than this. When you open the foil packet, the wonderful aroma that is released will nearly knock you out!

1. Heat a convection oven to 356°F.
2. Spread out a large piece of aluminum foil (large enough to make a foil packet around the fish), then place a sheet of parchment paper over the foil.
3. Cut the carrots into coarse chunks. Rinse and roughly chop the leek. Wash the lemon and cut into wedges. Place the carrot, leek, and lemon wedges on the parchment paper and add salt. Place the cod on top.
4. Make the dill butter. Use a pestle and mortar to grind the dill seeds and mix with fresh dill and butter in a bowl. Spread the dill butter over the cod.
5. Wrap the foil up over the cod into a packet and place on a pan in the oven. Bake for around 30 minutes.
6. Remove from the oven, open the packet, and sprinkle with salt. Serve immediately, preferably with a mixed green salad.

SERVES 4

1 bunch carrots, around 1 pound
1 leek
1 lemon
Around 1 teaspoon salt
Flaked salt
Around 1 pound cod fillets, skinless

DILL BUTTER

1 teaspoon dill seeds
⅔ cup finely chopped dill
1.75 ounces butter at room temperature

FISH BURGERS
WITH RED ONION AND GUACAMOLE

You don't need both salmon and cod in these burgers; you can use either one. You can also use more of one and less of the other if you prefer.

1. Heat the oven to 392°F, top heat.
2. Cut the salmon and cod into pieces and finely chop the chili. Put the fish, chili, egg whites, cilantro, dill, fish sauce, salt, and lime juice in a mixer. Mix until blended. Shape mixture into four burger patties and place on a pan lined with parchment paper. Brush with oil.
3. Peel the red onion and cut into 1½-inch slices to form onion rings (save some onion remnants for the guacamole). Salt the onion rings. Cut the limes in half and place the onion rings and lime halves on the pan with the burgers. Bake together in the oven for around 15 minutes.
4. Make the guacamole. Halve the avocado and remove the seed. Put the flesh into a bowl and mash with a fork. Dice the tomato and chop up the remaining red onion. Mix into the bowl with the avocado and add the finely chopped garlic, mixing as well. Add salt.
5. Remove the pan from the oven and squeeze lime juice from two roasted lime halves into the guacamole. Mix.
6. Assemble the burgers with bread, guacamole, onion rings and cilantro. Serve immediately.

SERVES 4

Around 1 pound salmon fillets
Around 1 pound cod fillets
1 red chili pepper
2 egg whites
⅕ cup chopped fresh cilantro
⅕ cup chopped dill
2 teaspoons fish sauce
1 teaspoon flaked salt
Freshly pressed juice from
   ½ lime
Oil for brushing

GUACAMOLE

1 ripe avocado
1 large tomato
1 garlic clove, finely chopped
1 teaspoon flaked salt
Juice from 1 oven-baked lime

ACCOMPANIMENTS

1 red onion
Salt
2 limes
4 hamburger buns, preferably
   brioche
1 large bunch cilantro,
   chopped

GIANT SHRIMP
IN SPICY CHILI SAUCE

Look for MSC (Marine Stewardship Council) or ASC (Aquaculture Stewardship Council) labels in the shrimp and any other seafood you buy. The labels guarantee that the product was sourced sustainably, both for the workers and the environment.

1. Heat the oven to 446°F using the grill function (bottom heat).
2. Cut the chili into pieces. Peel and finely chop the garlic.
3. Mix all ingredients for the spicy chili sauce in a bowl. Place the shrimp in the bowl, making sure they are covered by the sauce.
4. Place the sauced shrimp on a pan lined with parchment paper and roast in the oven for around 10 minutes, until they are cooked through and have a bit of color.
5. Remove the pan from the oven and serve immediately as a starter or canapé if you like. And why not add a glass of bubbly while you're at it?

SERVES 4

16 giant shrimp, uncooked

SPICY CHILI SAUCE

2 red chili peppers
2 garlic cloves
1 teaspoon sambal oelek
$\frac{2}{5}$ cup mango chutney
Freshly pressed juice from ½ lemon
½ teaspoon salt

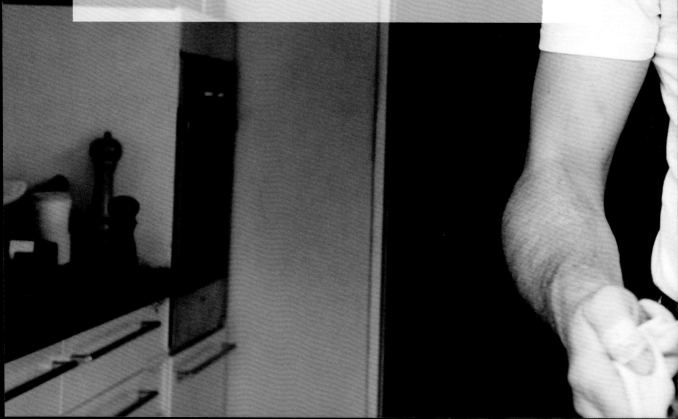

MEAT AND POULTRY

CHILI CON POLLO

This recipe shows the benefits of using an oven to cook your food. While it doesn't take any more time than it would on a stovetop, the flavors have more time to develop in the oven, making this chicken chili taste a lot better!

1. Heat a convection oven to 356°F.
2. Mix all the ingredients for the spicy tomato sauce in a bowl. Use a handheld blender to make a sauce with a smooth consistency.
3. Cut the chicken into 8 to 10 pieces and slice the chorizo. Peel the carrot and onion and cut into pieces. Halve the chilis lengthwise and cut the peppers into small bits.
4. Place the chicken, chorizo, vegetables, and beans in a roasting pan or large oven-safe dish. Pour the sauce over and mix.
5. Bake in the oven for around 1 hour and 15 minutes. Remove and serve immediately with a nice sourdough bread (optional).

SERVES 4

1 whole chicken
1 chorizo
1 carrot
1 yellow onion
2 green chili peppers
1 green bell pepper
1 red bell pepper
1 packet mixed beans, white, kidney, and black

SPICY TOMATO SAUCE

3 cups crushed tomatoes
2 tablespoons tomato puree
1 teaspoon ground cumin
1 teaspoon freshly ground black pepper
2 teaspoons chili powder
½ teaspoon chili flakes
2 cups water
3 teaspoons salt
Freshly pressed juice of ½ lemon

WHOLE CHICKEN WITH MEDITERRANEAN VEGETABLES

This is a really nice dinner with a French touch—made simple! Delicious with oven-roasted potato wedges.

1. Heat a convection oven to 356°F.
2. Roughly grate the summer squash, zucchini, and eggplant using a grater. Mix the vegetables with white wine in a bowl and pour everything into an oven-safe dish.
3. Pluck the rosemary leaves from the sprig. Mix together with the oil using a handheld blender. Massage the rosemary oil into the chickens and season with salt. Finally, add a generous amount of freshly ground pepper.
4. Place the chickens on top of the vegetables in the dish. Place everything in the oven and bake for around 1 hour and 20 minutes. Remove and make sure the chicken is cooked through. The juices should run clear and the internal temperature in the thigh should be 180°F. Serve immediately—roasted potato wedges make a great accompaniment.

SERVES 4

1 yellow summer squash
1 zucchini
1 eggplant
⅕ cup white wine
1 bunch rosemary
⅖ cup oil
2 whole chickens
1 teaspoon salt
Freshly ground black pepper

CHICKEN LEG CONFIT

Chicken confit ready to eat.

The term *confit* means cooking raw ingredients in fat, in this case oil. It's more common to use duck, but chicken works just as well.

1. Use a pestle and mortar to grind salt, sugar, allspice, pepper, and cloves. Peel and grate the garlic. Pluck the rosemary and thyme leaves from the sprigs. Mash and grind together the spices, garlic, and herbs in a bowl. Add the chicken drumsticks and rub them with the mixture. Leave them in the fridge for at least 6 hours, preferably overnight.
2. Heat a convection oven to 248°F.
3. Rinse the chicken drumsticks in cold water, mainly to remove the salt; some herbs can remain. Place the drumsticks in an oven-safe dish and pour enough oil over to cover them. Place in the oven and leave for around 4 hours.
4. Remove from the oven and separate the chicken from the oil (the oil can be kept and used to fry other things in).
5. Turn on the grill function (bottom heat). Place the drumsticks on a pan lined with parchment paper and grill in the oven just before serving, for 7 to 10 minutes, to crisp the skin. Remove and serve immediately. This works well with a mixed green salad, some tasty lentils, or mashed potato and pickled vegetables.

SERVES 4

4 tablespoons flaked salt
1 teaspoon granulated sugar
10 whole allspice
10 black peppercorns
5 cloves
1 garlic clove
1 sprig fresh rosemary
10 sprigs thyme
4 chicken drumsticks
Neutral oil, e.g. canola or
   sunflower oil

CHICKEN BREASTS WITH MUSHROOM, LEEK, AND RAW TOMATO SAUCE

Don't worry if the leeks catch too much color and get a bit charred around the edges—this just adds to the taste. The chicken skin also gets nice and crispy on the grill.

1. Turn on the grill function (bottom heat) and heat the oven to 392°F.
2. Place the chicken in a greased roasting pan. Place the mushrooms in the pan, caps down. Cut the leek into pieces and place them on their sides in the pan.
3. Add dollops of ricotta over the dish and drizzle with olive oil. Add salt, pepper, and lemon juice over everything. Grill in the oven for around 20 minutes.
4. Meanwhile, make the raw tomato sauce. Finely chop the tomatoes and peel and chop the onion. Mix the tomato with the onion, parsley, lemon juice, oil, and salt in a bowl.
5. Remove the roasting pan and pour the juices in the pan over the chicken, mushrooms, and leeks. Serve immediately with the cold tomato sauce and some arugula. If you want to make the dish a bit more filling, you can add some roasted potato wedges.

SERVES 4

4 large chicken breasts
16 large mushrooms
1 leek
3.5 ounces ricotta
Olive oil
Salt
Freshly ground black pepper
Juice from 1 lemon
Arugula to serve

RAW TOMATO SAUCE

2 large tomatoes
½ yellow onion
⅓ cup fresh, chopped flat-leaf parsley
3 tablespoons freshly pressed lemon juice
5 tablespoons olive oil
1 teaspoon flaked salt

HERB-CRUSTED PORK TENDERLOIN WITH TOMATO SALAD

I want to give a shout-out to tenderloin, which has been out of the limelight for a while. With a tasty herb crust, one is reminded why it was once so popular. Tenderloin is a nice cut that I both enjoy cooking and eating.

1. Heat a convection oven to 356°F.
2. Remove the fat and sinew from the tenderloin.
3. Peel the garlic clove and break the bread into pieces. Mix garlic and bread with parsley, tarragon, and chervil in a food processor. When the herbs have been broken up, add butter and salt and mix a little more.
4. Cover the tenderloin with the herb butter. Place on a pan and cook in the oven for about 30 minutes, until the internal temperature reaches 147°F.
5. Make the tomato salad while the tenderloin is in the oven. Cut the tomatoes into slices. Peel, halve, and cut the red onion into thin slices. Whisk vinegar, oil, mustard, honey, and salt in a bowl or shake the Dijon vinaigrette ingredients in a jar with a lid until it blends. Place the tomatoes and onion on a plate and pour the vinaigrette over.
6. Remove the tenderloin from the oven and leave it to rest; the inside temperature will continue to rise. Then cut into slices and serve warm, together with the tomato salad and, if you wish, the potato gratin with salsify and goat cheese from page 45.

SERVES 4

1 pork tenderloin
1 garlic clove
3.5 ounces white sourdough bread
⅕ cup flat-leaf parsley leaves
1 bunch tarragon
1 bunch chervil
2.5 ounces butter, salted
1 teaspoon flaked salt

TOMATO SALAD

4 tomatoes
1 red onion
2 tablespoons white wine vinegar
2 tablespoons neutral sunflower oil
1 tablespoon Dijon mustard
2 teaspoons liquid honey
1 pinch salt

PULLED PORK

Pulled pork has always been a favorite. These days, you can even buy it ready-made, but why not make your own? It is so much better! In addition, the meat doesn't need any attention while it cooks.

1. Heat an oven on a regular setting to 257°F.
2. Mix tomato puree, honey, vinegar, sambal oelek, salt, and water in a bowl.
3. Place the pork butt in an oven-safe casserole dish with a lid and pour in the tomato mixture. Lid the casserole and place in the oven. Leave it for around 4½ hours.
4. Make the pickled red onion. Peel and halve the red onion and cut into thin slices. Place in a bowl. Mix sugar, water, and white vinegar with a handheld blender separately. Pour the mix over the onion and leave for at least a few hours.
5. Remove the casserole from the oven and pull the meat apart with two forks. Mix the meat with the sauces in the casserole dish.
6. Place the meat on the bottom half of the hamburger bun, top with salad leaves, pickled red onion, and cilantro, and finish with the top half of the bun Enjoy!

SERVES 4

2 tablespoons tomato puree
2 tablespoons honey
2 tablespoons red wine vinegar
1 tablespoon sambal oelek
1 teaspoon coarse salt
1⅕ cups water
2.2 pounds pork butt

PICKLED RED ONION

1 large red onion
⅖ cup granulated sugar
⅖ cup water
⅕ cup white vinegar, 12%

ACCOMPANIMENTS

4 hamburger buns, preferably brioche
Mixed green salad leaves
1 bunch cilantro

PORK BELLY WITH
POTATO AND FENNEL BAKE

If you haven't tried pork belly before, now is the time. Once you've tasted this crispy rind, you'll never look back!

1. Score the rind, leaving ½ inch between each cut. Leave the rind to dry at room temperature for about 1 hour and wipe it down with some paper towels.
2. Heat the oven to 338°F, top heat.
3. Cover the flesh of the pork belly with salt all over. Place on the pan with the rind facing up and cook in the oven for around 1½ hours. Remove from the oven and leave it to rest while you make the potato and fennel bake.
4. Increase the temperature in a convection oven to 392°F.
5. Peel the potato. Remove the fronds from the fennel, and set aside. Cut the potato and fennel into thick slices. Peel and chop the garlic clove into thin slices. Place the potato, fennel, and garlic slices in an oven-safe dish with a lid. Sprinkle with salt and add wine. Add dollops of butter over the dish and top off with the bunches of fennel fronds. Lid the dish and place in the oven to bake for 25 to 30 minutes.
6. Meanwhile, cut the pork into slices.
7. Remove the dish from the oven and serve the pork immediately with the warm potato and fennel bake. Feel free to add a mixed green salad and some pickled red onion (see page 85).

SERVES 4

1 piece high-quality pork belly with rind, boneless (around 4.4 pounds)
Salt

POTATO AND FENNEL BAKE

Around 1 pound potato
2 fennels
1 garlic clove
1 teaspoon flaked salt
⅓ cup white wine
1.75 ounces butter

OVEN-BAKED PANCAKE WITH BACON AND LINGONBERRIES

This is a real midweek saver when everyone is hungry and crying out for food! You probably already have most of the ingredients at home—and if you don't have any frozen lingonberries, you can use lingonberry jam. You can also replace lingonberries with cranberries.

1. Heat a convection oven to 392°F. Grease a roasting pan.
2. Mix milk, flour, eggs, and salt in a bowl and blend with a handheld blender until smooth. Pour the mixture into the pan and bake in the oven for around 20 minutes.
3. Put the bacon on a separate pan lined with parchment paper and cook at the same time at the top of the oven but only for about 15 minutes.
4. Remove the pancake and bacon and put the bacon pieces on top of the pancake. Serve immediately with lingonberries (or lingonberry jam).

SERVES 4

Butter for the pan
2 pints whole milk
2 cups flour
5 eggs
1 teaspoon salt
5 ounces bacon (or 1 packet)

TO SERVE

Lingonberries, see page 97

"STUFFED" SAUSAGE TWO WAYS

"You can see how the sausage is "stuffed" two ways in the photo—and of course you can choose to use either one of them. This might be your family's new favorite dish!

1. Heat a convection oven to 320°F.
2. Peel the carrots and cut into pieces. Halve the leek lengthways, rinse, and cut into pieces. Place the carrots and leeks in a roasting pan. Mix with olive oil and salt.
3. Make incisions in the sausage, around ½ inch apart and a third through the sausage (not the whole way through). Place the sausage on top of the vegetables.

APPLE, ONION, AND MUSTARD FILLING

1. Cut the apple in half, remove the core, and cut into thin slices. Cut the onion in half and cut into thin, half-moon-shaped slices.
2. Arrange a slice of apple and onion together and stick in between the cuts made in the sausage. Spread or drizzle the mustard over and place the cheese on top.

TOMATO, ONION, AND OREGANO FILLING

1. Cut the tomatoes in half and slice into half-moon shapes. Cut the onion in half and cut into thin slices.
2. Arrange a slice of tomato and onion together and stick in between the cuts made in the sausage. Sprinkle the oregano over and lots of black pepper. Pour crushed tomato on top if you want the sauce to be more moist or saucy. Add the cheese on top.

BAKE IN THE OVEN

1. Place the roasting pan in the oven and bake for 25 to 30 minutes.
2. Remove from oven and sprinkle parsley on top. Serve immediately.

SERVES 4

2 large carrots
1 leek
1 tablespoon olive oil
1 teaspoon flaked salt
1 Bologna-style sausage ring (around 1.7 pounds)
Chopped flat-leaf parsley to garnish

APPLE, ONION, AND MUSTARD FILLING

2 apples
1 large yellow onion
1 tablespoon mustard
8–10 slices mature, hard cheese

TOMATO, ONION, AND OREGANO FILLING

2 large tomatoes
1 large yellow onion
2 teaspoons dried oregano
Freshly ground or roughly crushed black pepper
1 can crushed tomatoes, around 1 pound (optional)
8–10 slices mature hard cheese

CHORIZO WITH POTATO, TOMATO, AND ARTICHOKE

When the potato cooks in the tomato sauce, it imparts a deeper, more concentrated taste to the dish. The chorizo is important as it adds both fat and flavor.

1. Heat a convection oven to 356°F.
2. Peel the potatoes and cut into pieces.
3. Pour the crushed tomatoes on a baking pan and place the potato on top. Press the garlic over. Pluck the thyme leaves from the sprig, sprinkling them on top. Mix and bake in the oven for 30 minutes.
4. Meanwhile, cut the cherry tomatoes and artichoke hearts into halves. Cut the peppers into pieces and slice the chorizo. Remove the pan from the oven and place the chorizo pieces on top. Roast for another 10 minutes.
5. Remove the pan again and add the cherry tomatoes, artichoke hearts, and peppers. Roast in the oven for another 20 minutes.
6. Slice the olives. Remove the pan and top off with olives and lemon zest. Serve immediately.

SERVES 4

1.1 pounds potatoes
1 can crushed tomatoes, around 1 pound
2 garlic cloves
1 sprig fresh thyme
0.5 pound cherry tomatoes
1 can artichoke hearts, around 1 pound
1 yellow bell pepper
1 green bell pepper
7 ounces chorizo
Black olives, pitted, to garnish
Grated zest from ½ lemon

CHORIZO WITH
BAKED BEET AND GOAT CHEESE

It doesn't get simpler than this—chorizo, beets, goat cheese, and rosemary. Pop this in the oven and do something else while it cooks. Plus, it tastes amazing!

1. Heat a convection oven to 356°F.
2. Peel the beets, place on a pan, and bake them in the oven for around 1 hour.
3. Cut the beets into pieces and place them on a pan or in an oven-safe dish. Drizzle some honey and olive oil on top. Pluck the rosemary leaves off the sprig and sprinkle over the beets. Mix.
4. Cut a few slits in the chorizo and place them along the edge of the pan (like in the photo). Bake everything in the oven for around 15 minutes.
5. Remove from the oven and crumble goat cheese on top in good-sized chunks. Return to the oven and bake for another 5 minutes. Remove and serve immediately.

SERVES 4

4 large beets
2 tablespoons honey
3 tablespoons olive oil
1 sprig rosemary
3 chorizo
3.5 ounces goat cheese

CABBAGE PUDDING
WITH LINGONBERRIES

Cabbage pudding is an authentic, home-cooked meal that has been a staple in Sweden for a long time. I really want to revive it with this recipe. It is both easy to make as well as great-tasting. Cabbage pudding sometimes contains rice, but not in my version. If you can't find lingonberries, you can use cranberries.

1. Heat the oven to 392°F, fan assisted.
2. Cut the cabbage into small pieces and peel and slice the onion. Place the cabbage and onion on a pan. Add salt and drizzle with some syrup. Mix and bake in the oven for about 30 minutes. Remove the pan and mix the cabbage with white vinegar.
3. To make the ground meat, peel and finely chop the onion. Mix the onion, ground meat, allspice, pepper, salt, bread crumbs, milk, and eggs in a bowl.
4. Place half of the baked cabbage on the bottom of an oven-safe dish. Place the minced meat mix on top, and then add another layer of cabbage. Finish with a couple of dollops of butter on top and bake in the oven for around 30 minutes. If you want, place some foil on top after 15 minutes in the oven.
5. Meanwhile, put the frozen lingonberries in a bowl and mix with sugar. Leave them to defrost.
6. Remove the dish from the oven and serve immediately with lingonberries (or lingonberry jam).

SERVES 4

3.3 pounds white cabbage
½ yellow onion
2 teaspoons salt
⅖ cup light syrup
1 teaspoon white vinegar, 12%
1.7 ounces butter for the top

GROUND MEAT

1 yellow onion
1.3 pounds ground meat (mixed pork/beef)
1 teaspoon crushed allspice
1 teaspoon crushed black pepper
2 teaspoons salt
⅖ cup bread crumbs
⅕ cup whole milk
3 eggs

LINGONBERRIES

I packet frozen lingonberries, around 8 ounces
0.3 cup granulated sugar

MEATLOAF WITH
BACON AND ROOT VEGETABLES

Despite often being overlooked, meatloaf is adored by older and younger children alike—and even adults.

1. Heat a convection oven to 356°F.
2. Peel and finely chop 2 onions. Mix the onion, ground meat, allspice, black pepper, salt, bread crumbs, milk, and eggs. Shape the mixture into a loaf and place in the middle of a pan or in an oven-safe dish. Cover the loaf with bacon.
3. Peel the potatoes, carrots, and 1 onion. Cut the potatoes and carrots into thick slices and the onion into wedges. Place the vegetables around the meatloaf. Bake in the oven for around 1 hour.
4. Remove and serve immediately.

SERVES 4

3 yellow onions, divided
2.2 pounds ground meat (mixed pork/beef)
1 teaspoon ground allspice
1 teaspoon ground black pepper
3 teaspoons salt
⅖ cup bread crumbs
⅕ cup whole milk
3 eggs
Around 9.5 ounces bacon to cover the ground meat
4 large potatoes
2 large carrots

GROUND LAMB
WITH POTATO AND ZUCCHINI

My dad often made this dish when my brother and I were little. In my version, I grate the potato rather than slice it like my father did. Of course, the great flavor is the same—I'll never change that!

1. Heat a convection oven to 356°F.
2. Peel and roughly grate the potatoes using a grater. Place the grated potato in an oven-safe dish, add salt, and press it into the bottom of the dish.
3. Mix the ground lamb, parsley, grated garlic, lemon juice, water, and flaked salt. Place the meat mixture over the potatoes and spread the crushed tomatoes over everything.
4. Cut the zucchini in ¼-inch slices. Place the slices on top of the dish so they cover everything. Drizzle on some olive oil and add salt and pepper.
5. Bake in the oven for around 30 minutes. Remove and serve immediately.

SERVES 4

2.2 pounds potatoes
1 teaspoon flaked salt
1.1 pounds ground lamb
⅘ cup chopped flat-leaf parsley
2 garlic cloves, grated
Freshly squeezed juice from ½ lemon
⅖ cup water
1 teaspoon flaked salt
1 (16-oz) can crushed tomatoes
1 zucchini
2–3 tablespoons olive oil
Salt
Freshly ground pepper

ROAST LAMB
WITH ROOT VEGETABLES

If you make cuts in the lamb fat before cooking, the meat will become lovely and crisp in the oven. Make sure you don't cut the meat, just the fat.

1. Heat a convection oven to 356°F.
2. Make cuts in the meat, around ½ inch apart. Rub salt all over the meat and add some freshly ground pepper.
3. Halve the leek lengthwise and rinse it. Peel the carrot. Trim the fennel. Cut the leek, carrot, and fennel into slices and place in a greased roasting pan. Place the lamb on top of the vegetables. Halve the garlic bulb in the middle across the cloves and place the halves in the pan. Place in the oven and cook for around 1 hour.
4. Meanwhile, wash the potatoes and artichoke and cut them in half. Mix with olive oil and flaked salt in a bowl. Remove the roasting pan after 1 hour and place the potatoes and artichokes with the cut side up around the lamb. Pour water over and return to the oven. Roast for another 40 minutes.
5. Check that the meat has an internal temperature of at least 126°F. Remove and let it rest for 40 minutes; the internal temperature will rise slightly.
6. Just before serving, heat the roast quickly in the oven at a high heat, then remove and cut it into slices. To make the gravy, keep the juices from the pan and mix with lemon juice and olive oil. Taste and add salt and pepper. Pour the gravy over the meat and serve immediately with the root vegetables.

SERVES 4

1 roast lamb, with bone
1 teaspoon salt
Pinch freshly ground black pepper
1 leek
1 carrot
1 fennel
1 whole garlic bulb
1.3 pounds potatoes
1 pound artichoke
2 tablespoons olive oil
1 teaspoon flaked salt
1¼ cup water

GRAVY

3 parts juices from the sliced lamb
1 part freshly pressed lemon juice
1 part olive oil
Salt
Freshly ground pepper

PIES, PIZZAS, AND BREAD

NACHOS WITH CHEESE, AVOCADO, AND SWEET CORN

"A real weekend treat and absolutely delicious! Just don't expect there to be any leftovers."

1. Heat a convection oven to 410°F.
2. Halve the avocado, remove the seed, and slice.
3. Layer the avocado, tortilla chips, sweet corn, and grated cheese on a pan. Place the pan in the oven and leave for about 10 minutes until the cheese melts.
4. To make the avocado mash with lime, halve the avocado and remove the seed. Scoop out the flesh and place in a bowl. Mash with a fork and mix with lime juice and cilantro, and a little bit of grated lime peel if you like. Add salt to taste.
5. Remove the pan from the oven and use the warm tortilla chips as a "fork" to scoop up the mashed avocado. Tastes good with a cold beer!

SERVES 4

1 avocado
1 small bag tortilla chips, around 6.5 ounces
1 small can sweet corn, around 5.25 ounces
Around 1.2 cups grated cheese, any type

AVOCADO MASH WITH LIME

1 avocado
Juice from 1 lime
1 tablespoon chopped fresh cilantro
Finely grated lime zest to garnish (optional)
Salt

BROCCOLI QUICHE WITH BLUE CHEESE

Quiche comes in and out of fashion, but I think we can all agree on how good it tastes. Blå kornblomst is a Danish blue cheese that I really like, but you can also choose another blue cheese variety that is mild, creamy, and flavorful.

1. To make the pie dough, place all the ingredients in a mixer and blend together to make a dough. Leave in a cool space for at least 1 hour.
2. Heat a convection oven to 356°F.
3. To make the filling, chop the broccoli and leek into pieces and place on a baking pan. Add salt and drizzle over some olive oil. Bake in the oven for around 15 minutes.
4. Attach some parchment paper to the bottom of a springform pan and line the pan with the dough. Prick the dough all over with a fork. Place a piece of parchment paper over the dough, and add dried peas or rice on top (the weight of the peas or rice will allow the pie shell to hold its shape better as it bakes). Blind bake the pie in the lower part of the oven for around 15 minutes. Remove the parchment paper with peas or rice (they can be used the next time you make a quiche) and return the pan to the oven to bake for another 8 minutes or so.
5. Reduce to temperature in the convection oven to 302°F.
6. To make the egg mix, whisk eggs and milk and season with salt and pepper.
7. Add the cooked vegetables to the pie shell and sprinkle with tarragon. Crumble blue cheese all over the dish. Pour in in the egg mixture and return to the oven to bake for around 1 hour.
8. Remove from the oven and serve the pie hot or warm. This works well with a mixed green salad.

SERVES 4

PIE DOUGH

1¾ cups flour (about 0.5 pound)
4 ounces cold butter
½ teaspoon salt
2 tablespoons water

FILLING

0.6 pound fresh broccoli
1 small leek
1 teaspoon salt
1 tablespoon olive oil
1 tablespoon fresh chopped tarragon or 1 small teaspoon dry tarragon
2.8 ounces blue cheese

EGG MIX

5 large eggs
2 cups whole milk
1 teaspoon salt
Freshly ground black pepper

PEAR, GOAT CHEESE, AND ALMOND PUFF PASTRY

"Wild garlic (ramsons) grows all over southern Sweden. In this dish, we use the leaves, which have a strong taste of garlic, rather than the onion itself. If you don't have wild garlic, use ramps instead or a combination of scallions and garlic."

1. Heat a convection oven to 410°F.
2. Place the puff pastry on a baking pan that is lined with parchment paper. Brush the edges of the pastry with egg.
3. Prepare the filling. Place the scallions and wild garlic on the dough. Crumble cheese over it. Bake the tart in the oven for around 15 minutes.
4. Meanwhile, cut the pear, remove the core, and slice thinly.
5. Remove the tart and top it off with pears and almonds. Drizzle honey on top and serve immediately. This works well as a starter.

SERVES 4

1 chilled puff pastry, around
   0.5 pound
1 egg, whisked

FILLING

3 scallions
4 wild garlic leaves or ramps
3.5 ounces goat cheese
1 pear
Around 15 sweet almonds,
   roughly chopped
1 tablespoon liquid honey

ASPARAGUS AND BRESAOLA PUFF PASTRY

Bresaola is cured beef from Italy that used to be prepared in caves! The meat is added after the tart has been in the oven; if not, it will go dry in the heat. It was first imported to the United States in 2000, and you can now find bresaola in many stores. If you don't have bresaola, use prosciutto.

1. Heat a convection oven to 410°F.
2. Place the puff pastry on a baking pan that is lined with parchment paper. Brush the edges of the pastry with egg.
3. To make the filling, mix cheese, butter, and egg yolks in a bowl. Spread the filling over the dough and place the asparagus on top. Bake the tart in the oven for around 10 minutes.
4. Remove the pan from the oven, sprinkle over some pine nuts, and return to the oven for another 5 minutes. Remove from the oven and add bresaola and salad leaves on top. Serve immediately.

SERVES 4

1 puff pastry, around
   0.5 pound
1 egg, whisked

FILLING

5.25 ounces grated
   Västerbotten cheese (or any
   hard, mature cow cheese
   like aged cheddar or
   Parmesan)
1.75 ounces butter at room
   temperature
2 egg yolks
1 bunch green asparagus
1 tablespoon pine nuts
7 slices bresaola or prosciutto
Little Gem or romaine lettuce
   to garnish

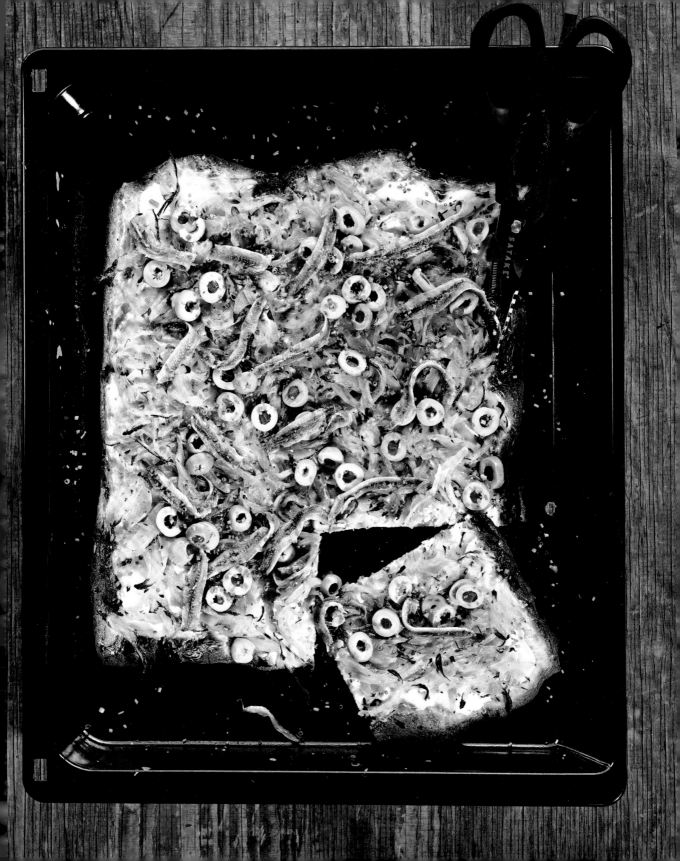

TARTE FLAMBÉE
WITH ANCHOVIES AND OLIVES

Tarte flambée, flatbread, flammkuchen, or pizza—this dish has been called many names. It is simply a thinly rolled-out dough that you add different toppings to and bake in a really hot oven.

1. Heat the oven to 527°F, bottom heat.
2. To make the filling, peel the onion and garlic and slice thinly. Fry in a pan with olive oil together with thyme until the onion is translucent.
3. With oiled hands, press the sourdough out on a pan. Bake in the oven for about 10 minutes until the dough is nearly ready. Remove and cool for 5 minutes.
4. Spread the crème fraîche on the dough and evenly distribute the onion mix on top. Place in the oven and bake for 10 minutes until the tart has gotten some color and the dough is crisp.
5. Meanwhile, finely cut the chives.
6. Remove the tart and top with chives, olives, and anchovies. Serve immediately as a starter or canapé.

SERVES 4

0.6 pound sourdough, see
   page 131

FILLING

1.1 pounds yellow onion
2 garlic cloves
Around 1 tablespoon olive oil
1 tablespoon chopped fresh
   thyme
7 ounces crème fraîche, 34%
1 small bunch chives
1.4 ounces olives, pitted
1 can anchovies, 2.8 ounces

NEAPOLITAN PIZZA
WITH ANCHOVIES AND CAPERS

"It's a good idea to invest in a pizza stone if you make pizza often—it makes the base of the pizza a lot more crisp and better tasting. Pizza with anchovies and capers is the best thing I know—so I always prepare this recipe!"

1. Blend flour, water, and yeast in a food processor for 3 minutes on low speed. Increase the speed and blend for another 5 minutes. Add the salt and blend for a further 4 minutes. Turn the dough onto a floured surface and divide into 6 pieces.

2. With floured hands, knead the dough pieces one at a time by pressing in the middle of the dough with the palm of your hand and then pulling the edges into the center. Repeat until you have a smooth, round dough ball. Carefully oil the balls on the top sides, cover with cling wrap, and leave to rise for at least 24 hours in the fridge (it can be left for up to 5 days).

3. To make the cold tomato sauce, peel the garlic cloves and cut the chili into bits.

4. Mix all the ingredients for the sauce to form a smooth consistency.

5. Heat the oven to 572°F on the grill setting (bottom heat). If you have a pizza stone, place it in the oven now so it can heat up.

6. Flatten each dough ball with your hands using lots of flour to make 4 medium pizzas. Spread the tomato sauce on top.

7. To prepare the filling, shred the mozzarella with your hands and place over the sauce evenly. Top everything off with drained anchovies and capers and finally some grated cheese.

8. Bake the pizzas one by one on a pan or the hot pizza stones until they get some color, around 3 to 5 minutes.

9. Remove from the oven and sprinkle arugula on top. Drizzle some olive oil over and crack a few rounds of a pepper grinder. Serve immediately.

SERVES 4

Overnight pizza dough
5½ cups flour (around 1.7 pounds)
2 cups water
0.25 ounce fresh yeast
0.75 ounce flaked salt

COLD TOMATO SAUCE

1 garlic clove
½ chili, any variety
1 can whole cherry tomatoes, around 1 pound
⅖ cup tomato pure
1 teaspoon dried oregano
1 teaspoon granulated sugar
1 teaspoon red wine vinegar
1 teaspoon salt
1 tablespoon olive oil

FILLING

1 buffalo mozzarella, around 4.5 ounces
1 can anchovies, around 2.75 ounces
Around 30 capers
⅖ cup grated hard, strong cheese
3.5 ounces arugula
2 tablespoons olive oil
Freshly ground black pepper

MARGHERITA PIZZA
WITH MOZARELLA AND BASIL

I make a warm tomato sauce for this pizza, but you can also use a cold one (see page 116), which is quicker to make. The warm tomato sauce also works well with pasta.

1. To make the warm tomato sauce, peel and chop the onion and garlic. Slice the chili pepper and celery.
2. Roast the garlic and chili in olive oil in a saucepan over medium heat until they turn golden. Add onion and celery and fry for another few minutes. Add wine and vinegar and leave to simmer until it is reduced by about half.
3. Add tomatoes and leave to simmer for another 45 minutes until it forms a thick sauce.
4. Add sugar and salt to taste. Sieve or blend the sauce until it is smooth.
5. Heat the oven to 572°F using the grill function (bottom heat). If you have a pizza stone, put it in the oven now to get it hot.
6. Use your hands to flatten each dough ball into 4 medium pizzas, using lots of flour for your hands. Spread the tomato sauce over each pizza.
7. To prepare the filling, shred the mozzarella into pieces using your hands and spread evenly over the sauce. Top off with grated cheese.
8. Bake the pizzas one at a time on a pan or on the warm stone until they turn a nice color, around 3 to 5 minutes.
9. Remove the pizzas and sprinkle with some fresh basil leaves. Drizzle some olive oil over and add freshly ground black pepper to taste. Serve immediately.

SERVES 4

1 overnight pizza dough
    (see page 116)

WARM TOMATO SAUCE

1 yellow onion
3 garlic cloves
½ red chili pepper
2 stalks celery
⅕ cup olive oil
1 cup white wine
1 tablespoon red wine vinegar
2 tablespoons tomato puree
2 cans crushed tomatoes,
    around 1.7 pounds
1 teaspoon granulated sugar
2 teaspoons flaked salt, e.g.,
    Maldon

FILLING

1 buffalo mozzarella, around
    4.5 ounces
⅖ cup mature, hard cheese
5–10 basil leaves
2 tablespoons olive oil
Freshly ground black pepper

WHITE PIZZA WITH PESTO, WILD GARLIC, AND ASPARAGUS

White pizza without tomato sauce has become popular in recent years. You can either use readymade pesto or make your own. If you don't have any pine nuts, use sunflower seeds instead. If you don't have wild garlic, use ramps or a combination of garlic and scallions.

1. Heat the oven to 572°F using the grill function (bottom heat). If you have a pizza stone, place it in the oven so it has time to heat up.
2. To make the pesto Genovese, mix basil, Parmesan, olive oil, garlic, pine nuts, lemon juice, and salt.
3. Using your hands and lots of flour, flatten each dough ball to make 4 medium pizzas.
4. To make the filling, break off the lower, hard part of the asparagus stalks where they break naturally.
5. Smooth around 2 tablespoons of pesto on each pizza. Add asparagus and wild garlic. Grate half a mozzarella ball over each pizza.
6. Bake the pizzas one at a time on a baking pan or on the warm pizza stone until they get some color, 3 to 5 minutes.
7. Remove the pizza from the oven and garnish with basil leaves and chives. If you like you can brush the edges with olive oil and season with freshly ground pepper. Serve and eat immediately.

SERVES 4

1 batch overnight pizza dough (see page 116)

PESTO GENOVESE

2 pots basil plant
⅕ cup grated Parmesan
⅖ cup olive oil, extra virgin
1 garlic clove, peeled
⅕ cup roasted pine nuts
Freshly pressed juice from 1–2 lemons
1 teaspoon flaked salt

FILLING

16 stalks asparagus
⅖ cup pesto Genovese (see above)
Around 20 wild garlic leaves or ramps
2 balls buffalo mozzarella, around 4.5 ounces each
1 bunch basil
Chives to garnish
Good quality olive oil for brushing (optional)
Freshly ground black pepper

WHITE PIZZA
WITH BLEAK ROE

Pizza with bleak roe—Swedish caviar also known as Kalix löjrom—is luxury of the highest order! Champagne is rarely served with pizza, but in this instance the pizza work perfectly with a glass of bubbly! You can also use other types of caviar if you don't have bleak roe—or substitute smoked salmon.

1. Heat the oven to 575°F, using the grill function (bottom heat). If you have a pizza stone, place it in the oven to heat it up.
2. Using your hands and lots of flour, flatten the dough balls into 4 medium pizzas.
3. To make the filling, wash and thinly slice the potatoes using a mandoline. Finely chop the chives. Remove the dill leaves from the stalks and shred the scallions. Peel and finely chop the red onion.
4. Take ⅕ cup of crème fraîche and smooth it over the pizza. Place the potato slices on the crème fraîche and spread the chives, dill, and scallions evenly over the potatoes.
5. Bake the pizzas one at a time on a baking pan or a warm pizza stone until they have some color, 3 to 5 minutes.
6. Remove the pizzas and add dollops of bleak row and the remaining crème fraîche on top. Finish off with dill and red onion and eat straight away. And don't forget the bubbly!

SERVES 4

1 batch overnight pizza dough
   (see page 116)

FILLING

1 small new potato
1 small bunch chives
1 small bunch dill
1 scallion (optional)
½ red onion
⅖ cup crème fraîche, divided
Around 2.5 ounces bleak roe
   or other type of caviar

CALZONE

Did you know calzone means "sock" in Italian? This is a folded pizza, where a filling of tomato sauce and ham is hidden inside the dough.

1. Heat the oven to 572°F, using the grill function (bottom heat). If you have a pizza stone, place it in the oven so it heats up.
2. Using your hands and lots of flour, flatten the dough balls into 4 medium pizzas.
3. Shred the ham.
4. Smooth the cold tomato sauce over half the dough. Place cheese and ham on the sauce. Fold the other half of the dough over the filling and pinch together the edges, like sealing a dumpling or pierogi.
5. Bake the pizzas one at a time at the bottom of the oven on a baking pan or a pizza stone until they have some color, 3 to 5 minutes. Watch out so they don't get burnt. Serve immediately.

SERVES 4

1 batch overnight pizza dough
  (see page 116)
Cold tomato sauce
  (see page 116)
6 slices smoked ham
1 buffalo mozzarella, around
  4.5 ounces
⅔ cup hard, mature cheese,
  grated

FOCACCIA

An Italian bread that originates from Liguria, focaccia is reminiscent of pizza. The bread works perfectly as a side, and you can choose to have many or few toppings on it. It's fantastic with just salt and rosemary, but also good with fillings like tomatoes, anchovies, cheese, and so on.

1. Mix yeast, water, flour, and salt in a bowl to make a loose dough. Leave it to rise under a cover or towel for around 30 minutes in room temperature, until the dough has almost doubled in size.
2. Heat a convection oven to 428°F.
3. Grease a roasting pan and place the dough in it. Press the dough against the edges of the pan with your fingers so it almost covers the pan.
4. Brush the dough with olive oil and make small holes in the dough with your fingertips. Sprinkle flaked salt over it. If you want to add fillings to your focaccia, feel free to use herbs, olives, tomatoes, anchovies, or cheese.
5. Bake in the oven for around 18 minutes. Remove and leave to slightly cool.
6. Break the focaccia into pieces and eat it as-is or slice it in half and fill it with something good for a sandwich.

SERVES 4

FOCACCIA BREAD

½ packet yeast, about
   1 ounce
2 cups water, at a temperature
   of 98.5°F
Around 5 cups flour, about
   1.5 pounds
2 teaspoons salt
Around ⅕ cup olive oil
Flaked salt to taste

TOPPING SUGGESTIONS

Herbs, e.g. rosemary, thyme,
   oregano
Olives
Sun-dried tomatoes
Grated cheese
Cherry tomatoes, halved
Anchovies
Feta cheese, broken in pieces

BAKING WITH A SOURDOUGH STARTER

In sourdough bread, the gluten in the wheat is broken down, and so thanks to this discovery, my family can enjoy sourdough without getting stomachaches. I've managed to keep my sourdough starter alive for the past four years.

Always weigh your ingredients when you bake—this will give you the best bread. Flour, for example, can fill different measuring vessels differently depending on how moist the air is; however, it will always weight the same.

I always use organic wheat flour, which is ideal for the lactic acid bacteria to thrive. You can replace some of the wheat flour with coarse rye flour to give the bread more "body." In the case of this recipe, use around 2.6 pounds (1200 g) of organic strong wheat flour and 0.6 pound of coarse rye flour (300 g). You can also Manitoba flour, which has a high gluten content, so use 2.8 pounds (1300 g) of wheat flour and just under 0.4 pound (200 g) of Manitoba flour to get a really nice bread with elasticity. You can also flavor the bread with dinkel, spelt, or Ölands flour as long as the ratio is 2.6 to 0.6 pounds (1200 to 300 g).

Every time you take from the sourdough starter, add some water and flour so there is always a bit left for the next time you bake. The finished sourdough starter should be kept in the fridge. Check on it now and again, but it does not need to be fed every day. If the liquid at the top starts to look a bit grey, discard it and add some new water, a bit of flour, and stir.

If you put some ice cubes or water (around ⅖ cup) on a pan at the bottom of the oven when you put the bread in the oven, you'll get a nice finish. Remember that the pan can buckle from the temperature difference, so don't use your best pan! You can also put a small casserole dish or bowl with water at the bottom of the oven. The steam from the water makes the surface of the bread soft and elastic, and it can rise quite a bit during baking.

Sourdough can also be used for tarte flambée (page 115) or for pizza.

BREAD TIPS

Score the bread with a sharp knife before you bake it.

Dust the surface of the bread with some flour to protect it from burning. The flour also shows off the pretty pattern better.

SOURDOUGH

If you prefer to bake the bread in a bread tin that's fine (see the photo). It makes it easier to toast the bread or use them to make hot sandwiches.

1. Peel and grate the apple. Mix the apple, flour, and water in a large bowl and leave at room temperature, preferably covered, for 3 days. Check in on it every day and give it a gentle stir. After 3 days it should bubble and have a sharp smell. If the mixture has separated, just add a bit more flour and stir.

2. Mix all the ingredients for the dough, except the salt, in a food mixer and mix at a low speed for 5 minutes. Add the salt, increase the speed, and mix for another 4 minutes. Move the dough to an oiled bowl, cover in cling wrap, and leave to proof in the fridge overnight or for at least 12 hours. If the dough rises over the edge, just fold it back down into the bowl.

3. Lightly knead the dough by folding it into the bowl—this retains the air in the dough. Fold the dough into the center from each corner a few times. Then divide the dough into 2 pieces. Fold the dough in on itself a few more times, each time folding the dough inwards from all four corners. Shape the bread and leave to proof on a baking pan or a bread pan at room temperature, covered, for 1 to 1½ hours. Heat a convection oven to 482°F.

4. Place 3 ice cubes at the bottom of the oven. Place the pan or bread tin in the oven and reduce the temperature to 428°F. Bake the bread until it has an internal temperature of 208°F, around 30 to 35 minutes.

5. Remove from the oven and leave the loaves to cool on an oven rack at room temperature. Cover them in a tea towel and place them in a plastic bag to keep their crisp crust.

2 loaves

SOURDOUGH STARTER

1 apple
Equal parts flour and water
e.g., 2 cups water and
2 cups organic flour

DOUGH

1.1 pounds sourdough starter
(see above)
2.2 pounds cold water
3.3 pounds strong organic
flour, or 2.6 pounds (1200
g) strong flour + 0.6 pound
(300 g) coarse rye flour
0.2 ounce (5 g) fresh yeast
1 ounce salt

HOT SANDWICHES THREE WAYS

When my brother and I were teenagers and went out surfing, our mother always made us sandwiches so we would be able to spend a long day at the beach. Often we would get an entire loaf each, filled with the same cheese mix that we use for Sandwich 1 here. If we were out overnight, the loaf would even last the entire next day, as well!

Heat a convection oven to 410°F.

SANDWICH 1

Mix cheese, egg yolks, and butter in a bowl. Spread thickly onto the bread. Bake until the sandwich has turned a nice golden color. Remove and eat immediately, although it also tastes good cold.

SANDWICH 2

Cut chorizo, pepper, tomato, chili, and onion into slices. Arrange the cut vegetables on the bread slices and place three slices of cheese on top of each slice. Bake until the sandwich has turned a nice golden color. Remove and eat immediately.

SANDWICH 3

Mix horseradish and mustard, and spread the mixture on the bread slices. Add ham and some scallion. Cover with three slices of cheese on each slice. Bake until the sandwich has turned a nice golden color. Remove and eat immediately.

SERVES 4

SANDWICH 1

- 2 cups finely grated cheese from the rinds + a bit of Västerbotten cheese (or any hard, mature cow cheese like aged cheddar or Parmesan)
- 2 egg yolks
- 1.75 ounces butter at room temperature
- 4 slices sourdough bread

SANDWICH 2

- 1 chorizo
- ½ red pepper
- 1 tomato
- ½ red chili
- ½ yellow onion
- 4 slices sourdough bread
- 12 slices hard, mature cheese

SANDWICH 3

- 1 tablespoon freshly grated horseradish
- 1 tablespoon Dijon mustard
- 4 slices sourdough bread
- 4 slices smoked ham
- 1 scallion, diced
- 12 slices hard mature cheese

WHILE THE OVEN'S HOT

FARMER COOKIES

I can never get enough of this classic! Prepare the dough and cover with plastic wrap, then keep it in the fridge (it will keep for over a week) or freezer. This way, you can bake as many cookies whenever you like when you have a craving or have visitors over. They also taste good crushed and sprinkled over ice cream.

1. Heat a convection oven to 392°F.
2. Whisk butter, sugar, and syrup in a bowl.
3. Mix flour, baking soda, and chopped almonds in another bowl. Mix this mixture into the butter mix to form a dough. Shape the dough into a roll, around 1¼ inches in diameter. If the dough gets too soft, place it in the fridge for a little bit.
4. Cut the dough roll into roughly ½-inch pieces and place them on one or several baking pans lined with parchment paper.
5. Bake in the oven for 6 to 7 minutes. Store in an airtight container in the fridge or in the freezer—they'll defrost in a flash.

AROUND 25 COOKIES

3.5 ounces butter at room temperature
⅖ cup granulated sugar
1 tablespoon syrup or honey
1¼ cups flour
½ teaspoon baking soda
0.3 cup chopped almonds

CINNAMON BUNS

These are probably the best cinnamon buns I've ever baked! The dough is incredibly fluffy and light, which is balanced by adding lots of butter and icing.

1. Dissolve the yeast and sugar in water in a food mixer. Add crushed cardamom and eggs. Mix everything and add flour. Mix on a low speed for 6 minutes.

2. Add butter, one tablespoon at a time, and work into the dough thoroughly. Add the salt, increase the speed, and mix for another 5 minutes. Put the dough into a bowl and cover with cling wrap. Leave to proof in the fridge for around 12 hours.

3. Tip the cold dough onto a floured surface and quickly roll it out into a large rectangle before it reaches room temperature. It can quickly become hard to work with due to the large amount of butter in the dough.

4. Heat a convection oven to 356°F.

5. Mix the ingredients for the filling in a small bowl. Spread the filling over the dough and then roll the dough into a thick roll. Cut the roll into 12 pieces and place the pieces on a pan that is greased or lined with parchment paper. Leave to proof until they double in size, at least 30 minutes.

6. Mix egg and water and brush the buns with the egg wash. Bake in the oven for around 30 minutes, or until the internal temperature reaches 205°F.

7. While the buns are baking, make the icing. Whisk butter, powdered sugar, and vanilla extract with an electric whisk. Add hot water a little at a time while you whisk it into a nice icing.

8. Drizzle the icing over the freshly baked buns and eat them straight away—they are so good! If by any chance you have leftovers, they can be frozen.

MAKES AROUND 12 LARGE BUNS

1.75 ounces yeast
⅘ cup granulated sugar
2 cups cold water
1 tablespoon cardamom pods, roughly crushed
2 eggs
2.2 pounds strong organic flour
7 ounces butter, room temperature
2 teaspoons sea salt
1 whisked egg + 1 tablespoon water for brushing

FILLING

2 tablespoons ground cinnamon
5.25 ounces butter at room temperature
Around ⅖ cup granulated sugar

ICING

4 tablespoons butter at room temperature
2 cups powdered sugar
1 teaspoon vanilla extract
0.3 cup boiling water

BLUEBERRY CRUMBLE

Don't defrost the frozen blueberries as they will stain the dough and make it blueish purple. Use them straight from the freezer—or use fresh blueberries for the crumble.

1. Heat a convection oven to 356°F.
2. To make the crumble, place oats, sugar, flour, and butter in a bowl and pinch into bread crumbs.
3. To make the blueberry filling, place the frozen or fresh berries in a roasting pan. Pour over the sugar, cornstarch, vanilla extract, and lemon peel and lemon juice. Distribute the crumble over the berries and bake in the oven for around 35 minutes.
4. Remove from the oven and serve hot or warm with a dollop of whipping cream or a scoop of vanilla ice cream.

SERVES 10–12

CRUMBLE

2 cups oats
⅖ cup granulated sugar
⅖ cup flour
3.5 ounces butter at room temperature

BLUEBERRY FILLING

1.1 pounds blueberries, frozen or fresh
⅖ cup granulated sugar
½ tablespoon cornstarch
2 teaspoons vanilla extract
Grated zest and juice from ½ lemon

TO SERVE

Lightly whipped cream or vanilla ice cream

CHOCOLATE LOVE CAKE

Love cake is a roasting pan classic that almost everyone adores. There are hundreds of recipes for love cake, but I think this one works best. Make it and serve your loved one the best cake in the world!

1. Heat a convection oven to 347°F. Place a sheet of parchment paper in a roasting pan.
2. Melt the butter in a saucepan or microwave, and leave to cool.
3. Whisk the eggs and sugar in a bowl until fluffy.
4. Mix flour, cocoa powder, baking powder, vanilla extract, and salt in another bowl. Sieve it into the egg mixture. Pour the mixture into the baking pan and bake in the middle of the oven for 20 to 25 minutes.
5. Remove the cake and leave it to cool to room temperature.
6. Meanwhile, to make the coffee icing, melt the butter. Mix with coffee, powdered sugar, cocoa powder, and vanilla extract until even. Smooth the coffee icing over the cake and top it off with shredded coconut. Cut into squares and serve with a cup of coffee—yum!

MAKES AROUND 20 PIECES

8 ounces butter
5 eggs
2 cups granulated sugar
2 cups (10.5 oz) flour
⅗ cup cocoa powder
1 tablespoon baking powder
1 tablespoon vanilla extract
1 teaspoon salt
⅘ cup whole milk
Shredded coconut to garnish

COFFEE ICING

2.6 ounces butter
0.3 cup strong coffee
2 cups powdered sugar
⅕ cup cocoa powder
1 tablespoon vanilla extract

FRUIT MERINGUE CAKE

This is my favorite cake. It is also known as brita cake, Margaret cake, Pinocchio cake, or manor cake. A soft sponge cake with a crispy meringue, cream, and berries, it is perfect to make for many people. You can either make one pan and divide the cake into two, or double this recipe to make two pans and combine the two cakes to make one giant cake.

1. To prepare the filling, hull and clean the strawberries and mix with the elderberry juice in a bowl. Leave for around 30 minutes.
2. Heat a convection oven to 356°F.
3. To make the sponge cake, mix butter and sugar with an electric whisk until light and fluffy. Add the egg yolks while you whisk. Mix flour and baking powder and add into the egg mix, then layer milk or cream over the mixture.
4. Place a lightly greased parchment paper in a roasting pan and pour the batter in. Smooth over the tops with a spatula.
5. To make the meringue, whisk the egg whites to make a stiff foam. Add the granulated sugar and vanilla extract. Smooth the meringue mixture over the cake batter. Top off with nuts and almonds and bake for around 20 minutes until the cake has some color.
6. Remove the cake from the oven and leave to cool. Slice it into two halves (unless you have made two large cakes by doubling the recipe).
7. To continue making the filling, whisk together the cream and powdered sugar.
8. Place one cake half (with the meringue facing upward) on a large plate or tray. Spread the strawberries on top and then the cream. Place the second cake on top (with the meringue facing upward). Serve immediately.

MAKES 10–12 PIECES

FILLING

1¾ cups fresh strawberries
⅕ cup concentrated elderberry juice
2 cups whipping cream
1 tablespoon powdered sugar

SPONGE CAKE

4.4 ounces butter at room temperature
⅖ cup granulated sugar
3 egg yolks
⅗ cup flour
2 teaspoons baking powder
About ⅖ cup milk or whipping cream

MERINGUE

3 egg whites
¾ cup granulated sugar
1 teaspoon vanilla extract

TOPPING

1¼ cup nuts and almonds, chopped

APPLE AND ALMOND-BUTTER SPONGE CAKE

Also known as Tosca cake, this dessert is popular in Sweden. When I added this cake to the menu at my first restaurant, it became so popular that people called us wanting to preorder a slice of cake with their coffee. Later on, after I baked the same cake on television, it became the most downloaded recipe in Sweden.

1. Heat a convection oven to 347°F.
2. Melt the butter in a saucepan and leave to cool slightly.
3. Whisk the eggs and sugar until light and fluffy. Add the egg mixture to the flour and vanilla extract and mix. Finally, add the melted butter and mix to form a smooth batter.
4. Attach some parchment paper to a springform pan and then grease and flour the pan. Pour the batter into the pan.
5. Peel and cut the apples into wedges. Push the pieces of apple into the top of the batter. Sprinkle some cinnamon over the cake and bake in the oven for around 25 minutes.
6. To make the tosca mix, melt the butter and sugar in a saucepan. Add almonds, flour, and milk.
7. Remove the pan from the oven and increase the temperature of the oven to 392°F. Pour the tosca mix over the cake and spread evenly. Return to the oven and bake for another 8 to 10 minutes until the cake has some color.
8. Serve the cake cold or warm with whipped cream, custard, or ice cream if you wish.

MAKES 8-10 PIECES

3.5 ounces butter
2 eggs
⅗ cup granulated sugar
⅗ cup flour
2 teaspoons vanilla extract
2 apples
Around 2 teaspoons ground cinnamon

TOSCA MIX

1.25 ounces butter
⅛ cup granulated sugar
1.25 ounces flaked almonds
1 tablespoon flour
1 tablespoon milk

TO SERVE

Lightly whipped cream, custard, or vanilla ice cream

BAKLAVA

In the Middle East and the Balkans, people often eat baklava as a dessert, preferably with a strong cup of black coffee. Baklava should be eaten at room temperature.

1. Heat a convection oven to 347°F.
2. Roughly chop the nuts and mix with the cinnamon in a bowl.
3. Melt the butter in a saucepan and brush the bottom of a roasting pan with a thin layer of melted butter, reserving most of it for later. Place a layer of phyllo pastry in the pan so it covers the bottom. Brush the pastry with some butter (the butter doesn't need to cover all parts of the pastry as there as several layers to brush). Add a new layer of phyllo pastry and brush with a little more melted butter. Continue until you have 10 layers of phyllo pastry (you should still have butter left over).
4. Place half of the nut mixture in the pan on top of the phyllo pastry layers. Then layer 10 more sheets of phyllo pastry on top of the nut mixture and brush a little melted butter between each sheet. Place the remaining half of the nut mixture on top of the phyllo pastry layers (reserve some chopped nuts for garnish). Finish off with another 10 sheets of phyllo pastry with butter in between to make a final layer. There should be a total of 30 sheets of phyllo pastry and 2 layers of nut mixture.
5. Press down on the baklava layers with your hand while you use a sharp knife to cut it lengthwise into roughly 1-inch strips. Bake in the oven until golden, for around 40 minutes.
6. Meanwhile, to make the sugar syrup, mix sugar, water, and lemon juice in a saucepan until the sugar has melted. Leave the sugar syrup to cool.
7. Remove the finished baklava and leave to cool for a bit before pouring the sugar syrup over—the cake should still be warm. Garnish with some chopped nuts and leave to cool in the pan at room temperature.
8. Using a sharp knife, cut strips of baklava in the size you want. Store in an airtight container in the fridge; they will last for a while. Before serving, remove the cake from the fridge and let it sit for a bit so it can reach room temperature.

MAKES AROUND 64 PIECES

1.1 pounds pistachios, walnuts, or sweet almonds
4 teaspoons ground cinnamon
9.6 ounces butter
2 packets phyllo pastry, around 1 pound

SUGAR SYRUP

3½ cups granulated sugar
1¾ cup water
Freshly pressed juice from 2 lemons

KANAFEH

Nabulsi cheese comes from the town of Nablus in Palestine and is similar to a hard mozzarella or a soft halloumi. If you use goat cheese, make sure it's fresh to get the right consistency. Kanafeh can also be made in a frying pan on a stovetop—in that case, just flip the cake over and pour the sugar syrup on top.

1. Heat a convection oven to 347°F.
2. To make the sugar syrup, mix water, sugar, and lemon juice in a small saucepan and cook until the sugar melts. Leave it to cool at room temperature and add rose water.
3. Melt the butter. Cut the kanafeh dough into 2-inch strips and place in a bowl. Finely separate the dough so that the "strings" are separate. Pour in the melted butter and carefully work into the dough—soft and easy! Leave the grainy remnants in the pan so there is less risk of creating lumps in the dough. Put to one side.
4. Discard the liquid from the ricotta by putting it in a colander to drain. Grate the goat or Nabulsi cheese and mix with the ricotta in a bowl.
5. Place half of the kanafeh dough in an oven-safe dish. Press the dough into the dish and place the cheese mix on top. Top with the rest of the dough.
6. Bake the cake in the oven for 30 minutes, covered with aluminum foil, then remove the foil and bake for a further 40 minutes.
7. Remove the cake from the oven and pour the sugar syrup on top, which should be at room temperature, over the freshly baked and warm cake. Decorate with pistachio nuts and serve immediately.

MAKES 8–10 PIECES

7 ounces butter
1 packet kanafeh dough, around 1 pound
1.6 pounds ricotta
8 ounces fresh goat cheese or Nabulsi cheese
⅔ cup pistachio nuts, chopped

SUGAR SYRUP

1 cup water
1 cup granulated sugar
2 tablespoons freshly squeezed lemon juice
1 teaspoon rose water

GRANOLA

What is the difference between granola and muesli? Muesli is made from dry ingredients, while granola contains some liquid and honey or sugar. It is then baked in the oven.

1. Heat a convection oven to 365°F.
2. Mix together all the ingredients from step 1 in a bowl. Spread evenly on a pan lined with parchment paper and put in the oven for 20 minutes.
3. Remove the pan and add all the ingredients from step 2 into the mixture. Place the pan in the oven again and bake for another 20 minutes.
4. Remove and leave the granola to cool. Store in an airtight container with a lid.

TIP

You can mix the granola with some dried fruit once it is finished and has cooled down, for example, shredded coconut, dates, apples, apricot, and so on. If you want the nuts to be roasted, you can roast them in the oven in advance at 302°F for around 20 minutes.

MAKES AROUND 7 CUPS

STEP 1

3½ cups oats
⅗ cup whole linseeds
⅕ cup granulated sugar
⅖ cup water

STEP 2

2 tablespoons honey
⅕ cup water
⅘ cup sweet almonds
⅘ cup hazelnuts
⅘ cup sunflower seeds
⅘ cup currants
1 teaspoon ground cinnamon

SALT-ROASTED NUTS

Nuts that are left to soak for a while before they are roasted taste better and are also healthier. When the water evaporates in the oven, a nice salty crust is created on the surface.

---

1. Mix salt and water in a bowl. Add the nuts and leave them to soak for 1 hour.
2. Heat a convection oven to 302°F.
3. Discard the water and place the nuts on a pan. Roast in the oven for around 20 minutes. Remove and leave to cool.

MAKES AROUND 2 CUPS

2 tablespoons fine salt
2 cups water
2 cups nuts of your choice, e.g., almonds or cashew nuts

CONVERSION CHARTS

Metric and Imperial Conversions

(These conversions are rounded for convenience)

Ingredient	Cups/Tablespoons/ Teaspoons	Ounces	Grams/Milliliters
Butter	1 cup/ 16 tablespoons/ 2 sticks	8 ounces	230 grams
Cheese, shredded	1 cup	4 ounces	110 grams
Cream cheese	1 tablespoon	0.5 ounce	14.5 grams
Cornstarch	1 tablespoon	0.3 ounce	8 grams
Flour, all-purpose	1 cup/1 tablespoon	4.5 ounces/0.3 ounce	125 grams/8 grams
Flour, whole wheat	1 cup	4 ounces	120 grams
Fruit, dried	1 cup	4 ounces	120 grams
Fruits or veggies, chopped	1 cup	5 to 7 ounces	145 to 200 grams
Fruits or veggies, pureed	1 cup	8.5 ounces	245 grams
Honey, maple syrup, or corn syrup	1 tablespoon	0.75 ounce	20 grams
Liquids: cream, milk, water, or juice	1 cup	8 fluid ounces	240 milliliters
Oats	1 cup	5.5 ounces	150 grams
Salt	1 teaspoon	0.2 ounce	6 grams
Spices: cinnamon, cloves, ginger, or nutmeg (ground)	1 teaspoon	0.2 ounce	5 milliliters
Sugar, brown, firmly packed	1 cup	7 ounces	200 grams
Sugar, white	1 cup/1 tablespoon	7 ounces/0.5 ounce	200 grams/12.5 grams
Vanilla extract	1 teaspoon	0.2 ounce	4 grams

Oven Temperatures

Fahrenheit	Celsius	Gas Mark
225°	110°	¼
250°	120°	½
275°	140°	1
300°	150°	2
325°	160°	3
350°	180°	4
375°	190°	5
400°	200°	6
425°	220°	7
450°	230°	8

INDEX

© Text Tareq Taylor, 2018. Photos Peter Carlsson, 2018

First English-language edition
English language translation copyright © 2019 Skyhorse Publishing

Original title *Mat på en plåt*
First published by Bonnier Fakta, Stockholm, Sweden
Published in the English language by arrangement with Bonnier Rights, Stockholm, Sweden

All rights reserved. No part of this book may be reproduced in any manner without the express written consent of the publisher, except in the case of brief excerpts in critical reviews or articles. All inquiries should be addressed to Skyhorse Publishing, 307 West 36th Street, 11th Floor, New York, NY 10018.

Skyhorse Publishing books may be purchased in bulk at special discounts for sales promotion, corporate gifts, fund-raising, or educational purposes. Special editions can also be created to specifications. For details, contact the Special Sales Department, Skyhorse Publishing, 307 West 36th Street, 11th Floor, New York, NY 10018 or info@skyhorsepublishing.com.

Skyhorse® and Skyhorse Publishing® are registered trademarks of Skyhorse Publishing, Inc.®, a Delaware corporation.

Visit our website at www.skyhorsepublishing.com.

10 9 8 7 6 5 4 3 2 1

Library of Congress Cataloging-in-Publication Data is available on file.

Cover design by Daniel Brount
Cover photo credit: Peter Carlsson

Print ISBN: 978-1-5107-5040-1
Ebook ISBN: 978-1-5107-5042-5

Printed in China